D1350892

THE
CAMPING
POCKET BIBLE

THE
POCKET BIBLE
SERIES

THE
CAMPING
POCKET BIBLE

CAROLINE MILLS

PB POCKET BIBLES

This edition first published in Great Britain 2011 by
Crimson Publishing, a division of Crimson Business Ltd
Westminster House
Kew Road
Richmond
Surrey
TW9 2ND

A catalogue record for this book is available from the British Library.

ISBN 978 1 907087 134

Printed and bound by Lego Print SpA, Trento

CONTENTS

INTRODUCTION

It's a late summer's evening, the sun is melting to a faint pink glow, and dusk is beginning to cast a magic spell over the campsite. There's a cheerful chatter in the background and the campfire crackles as it tinges the edges of a toasted marshmallow. Your campsite supper on the barbecue was a success and eating outdoors overlooking a great view added to the ambience of an enchanting evening.

Your tent is standing by; the warm and comfy bedding all laid out ready for a cosy night's sleep looks alluring in the torchlight. As sleep prevails over the campsite and that inimitable sound of tent zips echoes in the air, you climb under the soft blankets and allow the gentle sound of the breeze that rustles the tent canvas to send you off into a slumber.

In the morning you awake early to the sound of the birds singing a happy tune. Refreshed and raring to go, you find the sun is streaming through the tent, lighting up your canvas world and you can hear the sizzling of bacon drifting in from outside.

Camping is not just a weekend pastime: for many it is a way of life – and one that may have been instilled from a young age. Others come to it later in life, learning to appreciate the feeling of being at one with nature, out in the fresh air with the smells, sounds and senses of the outdoor world at your fingertips.

This world is explored within the pages of *The Camping Pocket Bible*.

With lots of explanations, hints and tips on selecting a tent and camping equipment, how and where to camp, choosing a place to stay, cooking and fun things to do, there is plenty to interest both the first-time and the experienced camper. Sections specifically exploring camping with children and enjoying the festival experience are included too. And, of course, lots of interesting facts connected with camping and being outdoors.

If you're new to camping, there's lots of information on what to expect and what you're likely to find at a campsite, and for more experienced campers, there's plenty to extend your thirst for living life under canvas either at a campsite or elsewhere.

However you enjoy camping, you can consider *The Camping Pocket Bible* a trusty friend, to dip into as and when required.

Happy camping!

YOUR CANVAS PALACE: ALL ABOUT TENTS

Visit any camping shop or exhibition where a selection of tents is on display and it appears to be a daunting sea of colours, shapes and sizes. What began as an exciting trip to buy a tent has turned into a disheartening mish-mash of ideas with too much choice. This chapter will guide you through the seeming maze of endless possibilities and help you to determine exactly which type of tent is right for you.

✺ BUYING A TENT ✺

There are hundreds of tent models available, but you can eliminate most of them providing you do a little preparation first to establish your needs.

Top ten hints before you buy

Before you even walk in through the door of the shop:

1. Know how many people are going to be using the tent most of the time.

2. Know the ages of the people that will be using the tent – very young children, teenagers, or adults only. Also consider the size and height of the people that will be using the tent – people over 6ft tall will have less choice owing to tent height and length.

3. Decide how you are going to carry the tent – backpacking, cycling or in a car. Weight is important.

4. Consider how many people are likely to be available to erect the tent. Weight is important here too, as is a tent's structure.

Single parents – if you're going to be the only adult in your family group, you need to think extra carefully about how you will manage erecting the tent on your own as this will influence the kind of tent you purchase. A lightweight, easily manageable tent will be necessary until your little ones are of an age to help productively.

5. Have clear in your mind where you are most likely to use the tent – at a campsite (what kind? see page 45), up a mountain, on an expedition etc.

6. Know when and how often you are going to use the tent – a guaranteed dry weekend in summer only, all year round, once a year for a fortnight, every weekend etc.

7. Know how you are going to use the tent – merely for sleeping in, socialising with friends, or playing games with family during wet weather?

8. Have some knowledge of tent jargon (use *The Camping Pocket Bible* to help) so that you don't feel vulnerable when reading tent labels and sales information.

9. Consider how experienced a camper you are. Some tent models are easier to erect than others and a basic, simple model may be less frustrating if you don't feel confident.

10. Have some idea of budget but be reasonably flexible – don't anticipate that you're going to be able to buy a tent suitable for an arctic expedition for a tenner in Tesco.

Having gone through this checklist, you should be able to eliminate the vast majority of the tents available as too big or small, too expensive, not suitable, too heavy etc, which leaves a select few that you can seriously compare.

Buying on the internet

Without having seen a tent, buying over the internet is a risky business. You really need to try out a tent, lie in it, stand up in it, decide how you'll live in it, see how easy or difficult the tent is to erect (and put away), or ask the shop to do so in front of you. You should also check the quality of the seams, zips and all other components. That's hard to do from a picture on a website.

However, if you want to buy a tent over the internet to take advantage of a special offer or because the supplier provides a better price or conditions, go and find one to look at and inspect first. Check that you're happy with it, then purchase one from your preferred outlet – whether that's online or in a store.

✲ HOW TENTS HAVE DEVELOPED ✲

The construction of recreational tents has moved on a long way since a piece of sheeting was draped over a length of rope and stretched between two poles. At least, it has in terms of the development of materials; you can still purchase tents that hark back to the humble beginnings of tent design if you so wish! And many of the more trendy-shaped tents that have been appearing on the market recently are returning right back to the traditional roots of nomadic camps in their design.

Advances in technology mean that the heavy steel poles and the very heavily oiled canvases of yesteryear have all but disappeared and tents have generally become lighter. You can now buy tents that weigh less than a bag of sugar, and while this is still heavy if you're climbing up – and back down – Mount Everest with the tent on your back, it's a very positive development.

Tent poles have also become more flexible now that materials such as fibreglass and lightweight metal alloys have been introduced into their construction. Even tripping over guy ropes in the dark has become a thing of the past thanks to modern designs.

Tent fabric

We may talk of sleeping 'under canvas', but more often than not tents are constructed using other materials these days.

Canvas, a kind of heavy cotton, is the traditional fabric of the leisure tent (historically, nomadic tents used whatever happened to be to hand, whether it was animal skins or palm leaves). The canvas is porous to begin with and requires rain to swell the fibres and knit them together to become waterproof. Being a natural material it breathes well but it can also rot over time, be incredibly heavy and needs quite a lot of maintenance to keep it in good condition.

Other, more modern materials have now replaced canvas in the manufacture of tents, such as:

- **Polyester**. A synthetic fibre that is more durable than nylon and the most commonly used in tent manufacture today.
- **Polycotton**. A mixture of polyester and natural cotton.
- **Nylon**. A synthetic material that is much lighter than either polyester or cotton, but is inclined to break down over time as a result of ultraviolet light.
- **TenCate**. The brand name of a cotton fabric coated with acrylic. One of the best tent fabrics; it is also one of the most expensive.

Once upon a time canvas was treated with oil or paraffin to protect it and provide a waterproof coating. All the materials used in tent manufacture today tend to be given a waterproof coating either of acrylic, polyurethane or a silicone impregnation. Acrylics are usually used on the cheapest tents that you can buy, while silicone offers the best protection.

Pocket Tip 🔥

Check to see if the tent material is fire retardant. Not all are and silicone impregnated tents are hard to make fire proof. If you're unsure it's safer to choose a material you can be sure is fire proof.

⊛ DIFFERENT TYPES OF TENT ⊛

To cut through the jargon, here's a guide to the most popular tent designs available today.

RIDGE

If you were asked to draw a simple sketch of a tent, what would it look like? Probably much the same as that used for maps and road signs: a triangular shape. It's the iconic design and represents the traditional ridge pole tent. Two rigid, upright poles are connected by a third (the ridge) and covered by a shelter. Guy ropes then hold the tent firmly in position. Ridge tents can be single or double skin (see the Jargon Buster on page 10 for an explanation), and can accommodate one to four people.

Advantage: Simple to erect

Disadvantages:

- Lack of headroom because of the sloping roof (maximum height only available along the ridge)
- Usually quite heavy, owing to the sturdy poles required
- Pole close to the entrance can get in the way of living area
- Hard to find now except second-hand

DOME

A dome is created using flexible poles in a half-moon shape, with the ends fixed to tapes at the base of the tent. These keep the tent roof rigid and the sewn-in groundsheet taut. Two poles crossing diagonally in the middle give a square floorplan; three create a hexagon. Dome tents require pegging down but may not need guy ropes. They can be single- or double-wall and can suit two to 10 people.

Advantages:

- Sides are more vertical so there is extra headroom across a greater surface area
- Good stability

- Small sizes are quick to erect and useful for a quick weekend break

Disadvantages:

- Larger sizes tend to be less stable and require guy ropes
- Smaller tents (for fewer people) have limited headroom

TUNNEL

Using flexible poles in the same semi-circular shape as a dome tent, tunnel tents differ in that the poles are lined up adjacent to one another to create a tunnel, with tent fabric in between. A useful shape, they can be used in a variety of floor-plans: a sleeping area at the back with a living area and porch at the front (door at one end); or sleeping areas at either side with a living area in the middle (door at the side). Usually tunnel tents are double-walled, requiring pegging and guy ropes. They are suitable for one to 10 people.

Advantages:

- Work well in high winds
- Good opportunities for windows and air vents, there is also more usable internal space than a dome tent
- Good height in larger models
- Look for designs where you can divide off the sleeping area in different ways, to utilise the space when used by families or different combinations of people

Disadvantage: Smaller designs provide limited headroom

GEODESIC

Evolved from the dome tent, geodesic designs have additional flexible poles that criss-cross the main poles to help support the structure. This makes them much more stable.

Advantage: Perform well in strong winds and snowy conditions as the additional poles help to prevent the fabric from sagging under the weight of snow

Disadvantage: To perform well in high wind they tend to be no more than four or five feet high, so headroom is compromised

Pocket Fact 🏕

Tent styles have influenced architecture over the years – such as the Sametinget or Sami Parliament building in Karasjok, Norway. Opened in 1989, it is shaped like the lavvo: *a Sami summer tent.*

VIS-À-VIS

A French term meaning 'face to face', these tents are usually a hybrid combination of a dome and two tunnel tents, providing separate sleeping areas either side and a living space in between. A porch area may also be included.

Advantages:

- Useful for keeping sleeping areas clean and for 'living' in
- Good for friends or a family who need separate sleeping spaces

Disadvantages:

- Can be quite long – check the footprint to make sure it will fit onto a standard pitch size
- Unnecessary for couples (unless there's an argument over dinner!)

FRAME

One for longevity, frame tents still use rigid steel poles to create a free-standing frame, over which the tent fabric is fitted. This is usually a canvas or coated polyester. Inside, an additional, lighter-weight inner tent creates the living and sleeping areas. They are the largest tents you can buy, and are much more home-from-home – with several sleeping areas, a large living space, and even possibly a porch. Frame tents now tend to be available only in larger sizes, normally for six to eight people.

Advantages:

- Near vertical walls, so great headroom across the floorplan

- Structurally sturdy, they are very roomy and therefore offer comfortable living

- Good for large families/groups of friends and for long stays at a campsite

Disadvantages:

- Very heavy and bulky to transport

- Take the longest time to erect of all the tent designs

- Not good for short breaks

TEPEE (OR TIPI)

Aside from the ready-erected 'authentic' canvas tepees that are available to rent on 'glamping' sites, the tepee shape has also come into fashion for more general camping. They are head-turners at festivals and on campsites, and provide alternative living space and separate sleeping areas. A central pole helps to keep the tent upright and some come with an extension for a porch too. Bear in mind that some models may not come with a sewn-in groundsheet.

Advantages:

- One for the style-conscious

- The shape makes it feel cosy inside

- Can have good ventilation through the top of the tent when a hole is made and a 'Chinese hat' is placed over the top

Disadvantages:

- Can be heavy and cumbersome to erect, requiring two people

- Not the most space-efficient

PUPS AND POP-UPS

Pup tents were originally small ridge tents, but the name has stuck to cover any very small, lightweight, single pole tent for one or two people.

Pop-up tents use a very flexible, springy, built-in hoop which, when unpacked, pops up into shape immediately. They tend to be very lightweight and are usually a single skin. They do require pegging down and are only suitable for one or two people.

Advantages:

- Lightweight

- Very easy to erect (the pop-up does it all for you)

- Good for festivals, children (independent teenagers enjoy their own space), and dry weather conditions

- Great when you need to add an extra couple of sleeping 'berths' occasionally, without upgrading an existing tent

- Generally inexpensive to buy

- Also useful as a dog kennel!

Disadvantages:

- Pop-ups can be a pain to put away

- Structurally not suitable in strong winds

- May not be very waterproof (most pups and pop-ups are designed for fair weather camping)

- Limited headroom

BIVOUAC

Also called 'bivys' for short, the smallest 'tent' you can buy is little more than a large rain cape that covers a sleeping bag for one person only. Used by the military, for expeditions, and by anglers.

Advantages:

- Extremely lightweight

- Helps to insulate a sleeping bag

- Good for backpackers

Disadvantages:

- Quite specialist
- Requires breathable fabrics in construction or condensation can form, making the sleeping bag damp
- Rarely covers the head

Tent manufacturers

Here are some major tent manufacturers and brands to look out for when you're searching for the perfect tent:

Berghaus: *www.berghaus.com*
Cabanon: *www.cabanon.com*
Coleman: *www.coleman.eu*
Gelert: *www.gelert.com*
Khyam: *www.khyam.co.uk*
Outwell: *www.outwell.com*
Royal: *www.royal-leisure.co.uk*
Sunncamp: *www.sunnflair.com*
Tentipi: *www.tentipi.co.uk*
Vango: *www.vango.co.uk*
Vaude: *www.vaude.co.uk*
Wynnster: *www.wynnster.co.uk*

Don't forget that most outdoor stores also sell own-brand equipment too.

✦ JARGON BUSTING ✦

There are all sorts of words that you're likely to come across when looking for a tent:

Air vent
This is necessary to prevent condensation from building up and to stop the tent from getting damp or going mouldy. All tents

need one, but any vents, windows, and doors then need to be covered with an ultra-fine mesh to prevent mosquitoes and other biting insects from entering the tent.

Pocket Tip 🔥

Tents can get very warm in summer and you will want some kind of ventilation at night. Check that windows and doors can be rolled back and held in place using ties or tapes.

Double skin

A tent that has two layers of fabric. The inner layer provides the envelope in which to live and sleep and is not necessarily waterproof, while the outer layer provides protection from the elements. The two should be kept separate, using spacers to avoid condensation appearing on the inner tent.

Pocket Tip 🔥

Look for designs that include small pockets sewn into the inner tent for torches, wallets and watches. They're very useful for keeping belongings orderly, especially when searching for something in the dark.

Flysheet

A waterproof sheet that is suspended over the tent clear of the roof (hence it 'flies'). Sometimes used to describe the outer skin of a double-skinned tent (although strictly this is incorrect).

Pocket Tip 🔥

Make sure that the flysheet is clear of the tent by using extra tent poles.

Footprint/Floorplan/Berths

This refers to the ground size of the tent and how many people it is designed for. Tent manufacturers describe their tents as being '2-berth' or a '3-person' tent. The tent label may show symbols of the number of adults and children it is suitable for. This is based upon the number of people laid down with a sleeping bag only and without room for airbeds, personal belongings, or living area.

Pocket Tip 🔥

Buy a tent that indicates at least two additional berths more than the number of people actually using the tent in order to provide sufficient space for equipment and living.

Groundsheets

These are generally sewn in to most tents these days to provide a complete watertight envelope. Rather than fitting on the ground only, a sewn-in sheet should come up the walls of the tent a little to create a totally watertight space.

Pocket Tip 🔥

Protect your groundsheet so you don't have to buy a new tent if it gets damaged (see page 18).

Guy ropes

Extension ropes, usually made of synthetic cord, to help steady the tent and hold it to the ground. They require some form of adjustment to keep the right tension, and, if required, will usually be attached to the flysheet during manufacture.

Pocket Tip 🔥

If the guy ropes do not include a light-attracting property in them, attach fluorescent markers up their length to be able to see them in the dark with a torch (before you trip on them).

Porch/Canopy/Vestibule

Many tents will include some kind of open canopy or porch area that can increase your outdoor living space, especially when it's wet, provide somewhere to kick off dirty wellies, and can be useful for cooking if you get wet weather as you should not cook inside the tent (see page 117). Side canopies provide additional protection from the elements.

Pocket Tip 🔥

Larger families can mean larger tents, and a porch is a godsend to have somewhere to entertain the children on rainy days — especially if the campsite doesn't have facilities such as a games room.

Single skin

A tent made using just one layer of waterproof fabric. Many of the most inexpensive tents are constructed in this way but, equally, so are the most expensive expeditionary tents that need to keep weight down. The quality of the fabric and waterproofing will be different though!

Pocket Tip 🔥

When buying an expedition tent, think about the choice of colour. Red and yellow are far more visible in the event of emergencies and the need to be seen.

Tent pegs

Used to anchor the tent and guy ropes to the ground, tent pegs can be made of metal, wood or plastic. They keep the groundsheet in position and help to prevent the tent from blowing away in the wind. They should be driven into the ground at an angle to maintain strength and should be checked daily to make sure that they have not become raised out of the ground through movement; a protruding peg is damaging to your tent and dangerous to tread on.

Pocket Tip 🔥

Buy fluorescent or coloured tent pegs that you can see in the dark and be noticed more easily upon removal.

Tent poles

These are either rigid steel for frame and ridge tents, or flexible for other designs. The cheapest tents will use fibreglass for the flexible poles but the more expensive metal alloys are more durable and tend to be stronger. Flexible poles are usually made in sections approximately 30cm long with sockets at one end to connect into one another. Elastic or cord is often threaded through to hold them together. Some tents even use inflatable airbeams, rather like a bicycle tyre, that is pumped up in place of poles.

Pocket Tip 🔥

The elastic in flexible poles can become brittle, stretch, and snap over time, and the poles themselves can snap, particularly when cold. Take spare cords and some gaffer tape with you in case you need to make repairs.

Waterproofing

Rain resistance is measured as a hydrostatic head in millimetres, and tents will be given a rating according to how waterproof they are. A rating of 1,000mm is just about shower resistant; 1,500mm is suitable for summer camping; 2,000mm for all-year-round use; and 3,000mm for expeditions. Tents may also be rated as 'one season' (summer), 'two or three season' (spring/summer/autumn) or 'four season' (all year). Those described as 'festival' tents are generally only showerproof.

Pocket Tip 🔥

You can reproof an old tent using a product such as Fabsil if it starts to lose its waterproofing qualities.

Zip

Obvious enough, but the best tents will have a double zip so that the door can be unzipped from the top or bottom.

Pocket Tip 🔥

Do not use detergents (including washing-up liquid) to clean your tent zips. The detergent may aggravate the waterproof coating of your tent if it's splashed.

✸ HOW AND WHERE TO ✸ PITCH A TENT

There are too many makes, models, and styles of tent to include an exact 'how-to' guide for pitching a tent, but there are some basic pointers that everyone can follow.

- Before you go camping, erect your new tent at home (or practice on a playing field, common ground, or a friend's garden if you don't have the space). Follow the instructions carefully and make sure that no pieces are missing. You don't want to arrive at a campsite in the dark having never pitched the tent before.

- On a campsite, check the ground around the pitch for tent pegs left behind and remove them before pitching your tent, or you may find that they push a hole into your groundsheet, or make your bed very uncomfortable.

- If you're wild camping or staying on a campsite without designated pitches, find ground that is flat. If there is a slight gradient, pitch the tent with your head uphill for a better night's sleep.

- You can move a few stones or twigs in order to find a flat piece of ground, but don't start uprooting plants to give yourself a clear pitch. Remember, things that were already there before you – plants, animals etc – have first priority.

- Think about your safety when pitching – don't set up right on the banks of a watercourse that could give way, into the prevailing wind, or directly beneath a rock face where stones or boulders could fall.

● Some tents require the flysheet or outer tent to be pitched first before the inner tent. Others reverse the principle. Check before you begin erecting the tent.

First time camping in a tent

If you've never been camping before, and you're not sure if it's the kind of holiday for you, it can be difficult to justify spending lots of money on a good tent and all the paraphernalia associated with camping. However, you can rapidly be put off camping altogether by buying a cheap and nasty, poor quality tent where the zip jams with the fraying threads and the zip puller comes off in your hand the first time you use it, or when you find yourself wet through with the inexpensive 'waterproof' jacket you bought. Ideally you need to try before you buy.

One solution is:

● *Buy the cheapest tent you can possibly buy. You can now purchase a three-man tent for under £20 in the large supermarkets. They are little more than play tents and you need to expect things to go wrong – such as ripped seams, poor-fitting zips, cheap poles, a potentially bad design that takes a little longer to erect, etc – reminding yourself that a better quality tent will not (or shouldn't) have these snags.*

● *Put the tent up in your garden and sleep in it for two nights. Don't buy any other equipment but use what facilities you already have at home. It will only give you a basic idea of camping, but if you don't enjoy waking up under canvas you're not going to enjoy any of the other aspects of camping.*

● *If you do enjoy the experience and decide that you would like to go camping properly, use the tent as a springboard for* what you might need to camp properly: deciding whether it was too small or too big and what you did and didn't like about it, and what snags or problems to look out for when buying your 'real' camping tent. Only then should you purchase a good quality tent and the other essential camping equipment that you need.

- Keep the 'tester tent' as a play thing for the children in the garden.

The alternative is to hire a tent and camping equipment and go to a campsite nearby. Companies such as Contented Camping (www.contentedcamping.co.uk) or Tent 2 Hire (www.tent2hire.co.uk) hire out tents and equipment so you don't have to spend a fortune unnecessarily. Hiring a tent is also a useful option if you think you're only going to go camping once a year or you don't have the space at home to store any camping equipment.

2

WHAT TO TAKE: ESSENTIAL EQUIPMENT

Camping can be a really fun, exciting, and exhilarating experience if you have all the right gear with you. Otherwise it's a miserable few days when you've got either poor quality gear or the wrong equipment to hand. Planning ahead can make all the difference. This chapter profiles all the essentials that you need to have to ensure you have an enjoyable trip.

✴ FOR SLEEPING ON ✴

So you've got your tent and it feels very cosy when you pop your head inside to take a look, but what about sleeping in it? Some people like a hard mattress, but very few would wish to sleep straight on the ground without some padding beneath them. Start from the ground and work upwards, beginning with the groundsheets.

GROUNDSHEETS

Most tents now include sewn-in groundsheets, but double check in case you need to take a separate one. Treat the groundsheet merely as a draught excluder and give yourself and your tent some extra protection. It will save your tent from lots of wear and tear and will make it last longer.

Beneath the tent

You really need to keep the base of your groundsheet clean so that when you pack the tent away in its bag you don't cover the 'walls' with mud and grass. Buy a tarpaulin from a DIY store or builders' merchants and place this beneath your tent to protect the sewn-in groundsheet. The additional layer will also help to prevent the cold from being drawn up from the ground, and so boost the insulation in your tent.

You can then pack your tent away, knowing that it has been kept clean and you don't have to try and wipe it down carefully. Keep the dirty tarpaulin separate in its own bag and wash off any mud and grass as soon as you get home. Leave it to dry before packing away ready for next time.

In porch areas

If you need separate groundsheets for porch areas, look out for the kind that lets the light and air through, allowing the grass beneath to breathe. Being breathable, they're not necessarily waterproof, but they can help to keep the mud and grass out of your tent and the pitch in reasonable condition for the next occupants.

Inside the tent

Some mud, dust, and grass always seem to find their way into tents. To save you the job of having to clean the inside of the tent too, you can cover the sewn-in groundsheet with another protective layer internally. This can be a picnic rug with a waterproof backing, or something similar. Used like a carpet in the tent, it will make the tent feel cosy and warm, especially when camping in autumn or on chilly nights, and can double up as intended – as a picnic rug on sunny days.

SLEEP MATS AND MATTRESSES

Getting a good night's sleep when camping can make all the difference as to whether you actually enjoy the experience or say, 'never again' in the morning. A hard, lumpy base and lying awake all night feeling the cold is likely to leave you saying the latter. Comfort is of the essence when camping. Who enjoys being grumpy, or being next to someone who's grumpy, in the morning? The answer is to put something comfortable between you and the ground.

There are several choices of 'mattress' to put beneath you while camping:

Sleeping mats

The simplest and least expensive option is a thin foam mat. This is the best option for backpackers as it rolls up tightly and can be carried with your rucksack. The more expensive mats are made up of complex layers of different types of foam, to give a more comfortable night's sleep.

'Self-inflating' mats

Great space-saving sleep mats, these offer the most comfort for limited travelling space; ideal if you're going camping in a small car. They can also be used by backpackers and offer more comfort than a conventional foam sleeping mat. Unroll the mat, open the air valve, and it inflates itself – so there is no need to huff and puff, making you so tired that you're ready for bed the instant it's inflated! You may need to top up the pressure a little over time, but most are surprisingly comfy with soft fillings.

Pocket Tip ☀
You can also buy self-inflating pillows, which can be used as a chair or cushion too.

Conventional airbeds and mattresses

These are simple airbeds; exactly the kind of thing you might buy when an extra guest is staying in your home. They can be bought for a few pounds, but if you can afford the extra for a better quality airbed, do so, as the cheapest ones can be inclined to leak air – meaning you need to top up the air pressure quite regularly. The latest models can be quite complex, with sophisticated inner construction to create a more comfortable night's rest. You can buy double bed-sized models too, or single beds that can zip together.

The downside of these is that they are bulky when rolled up and quite heavy; consequently, if you need several for a family, they can take up a lot of room in the car in comparison to sleeping mats. They do, however, create the most home-from-home comfort.

When buying airbeds, check that they are a standard size if you want to use fitted sheets and bedding rather than sleeping bags. Some airbed manufacturers also sell fitted sheets sized to match their airbeds.

Standard mattress sizes (cm) are:

- Single: 190 × 90 × 30

- Double (Queen): 190 × 135 × 30

- Double (King): 200 × 150 × 30

Pumps for airbeds

The last thing you want to do when you arrive on a campsite is to huff and puff to blow up several mattresses, so an air pump is essential if airbeds are your preferred choice. Hand and foot pumps are the most basic (and therefore the least likely to go wrong), but you can also buy an electric blower that will do the job for you using its own power supply (from batteries or a rechargeable power source). You can also buy pumps that plug into the 12V socket of your car. These are great providing you have a long enough lead to reach from the car to where you're blowing up the airbed. They're problematic if you're staying on a campsite that asks for cars to be left in a car park, away from the tent pitches.

If you can, look for a pump that sucks air out as well as blows air in, to make the job of deflating your mattress easier.

CAMPBEDS

Once upon a time campbeds, constructed from heavy metal frames, could be as weighty as the tent itself. Now they can be made from lighter materials, but still retain the strength and rigidity in the frame that is required.

Pocket Tip 🔥

A good test for rigidity is to check that you can sit on either end of the campbed without it throwing you onto the floor.

The design of a campbed is usually always the same: a canvas sleeping area stretched tightly over a collapsible metal frame. The canvas generally provides good comfort and has the advantage of being off the ground, so air can circulate beneath your bedding and body and doesn't draw in the damp.

The disadvantage of a campbed is that they are not normally very wide, so there's little room for spreading out. That's not a problem for a small child, but for a fully-grown adult of moderate proportions, turning over in a confined space takes some ingenuity without catapulting yourself onto the floor.

Campbeds fold up to be quite compact for travelling (although they are of course not as neat as a rolled up sleep mat), but you should check out various models both for comfort when extended and for compactness when folded up. Also check, if you need several, that they will all fit into the car.

Pocket Tip 🔥

Place upturned jam-jar lids under the campbed feet to protect the groundsheet.

✳ FOR SLEEPING IN ✳

Feeling cosy and warm under canvas can be one of the best feelings in the world; feeling cold can make a long night even longer. Keeping warm is necessary to enjoy a good holiday at a campsite, and it's absolutely essential for survival part way up a mountain with no opportunity to take shelter.

SLEEPING BAGS

The simplest (and generally least expensive) sleeping bags are rectangular in shape. They come in various sizes, from children's to double bed size. It's also possible to zip two single-sized bags together to create a two-person bag.

Some rectangular bags include a hood for your head to create a pillow, and also to keep your head warm.

Tapered or mummy-shaped bags are designed to be more snug, fitting more to your body than a rectangular bag – meaning that they maintain warmth as they have less internal space to keep warm. They tend to be more compact when packed and are therefore ideal for backpackers. Nearly all mummy-shaped bags include a hood for your head.

Mummy-shaped sleeping bags tend to keep you the warmest but they can also feel quite claustrophobic if you like to spread out. These are best for winter camping, although you can buy lighter-weight ones for summer.

Pocket Fact 🏕

Your body loses most of its heat through your head and to keep warm at night you need to keep it warm, so use the hood of your mummy-shaped bag or wear a hat. Similarly, if you are too hot (which can then cause stuffiness and headaches) you need to create some fresh air around your head and keep it cool. Remove any hoods or hats and keep your head close to an air vent within the tent.

How a sleeping bag works

A sleeping bag works by trapping warmed air inside its insulating filling. The insulated filling is one of the most important aspects of the bag, as this is what is going to keep you warm. Put simply, the more insulation you have around you, the greater the warmth. However, there are many factors that affect the performance of a sleeping bag including the local temperature and climate, the additional insulation that you have beneath you, the altitude, and personal factors such as how easily you feel the cold.

Natural insulating materials used in the manufacture of sleeping bags include the down from birds – with ducks and geese providing the best. They're great in luxurious duvets on your bed at home but in a sleeping bag, where there is a possibility of the down becoming wet and therefore compact, they're not so good.

Synthetic materials, such as polyester fillings, are better for sleeping bags. They have some resistance to damp and are quicker to dry should they get wet. They are also better for those with allergies to down and feather.

The outside fabric of the sleeping bag needs to be reasonably weatherproof, but it also needs to enable the bag to breathe so it does not become damp inside.

Pocket Tip 🔥

Try to air your sleeping bag whenever you can, to get rid of moisture.

Choosing a sleeping bag

- **Decide what kind of sleeper you are**. Do you feel the cold at night? Do you feel claustrophobic if there is little space to move around you?

- **Decide where you will be camping**. At a campsite in the UK or somewhere with a temperate climate; at a campsite with alternative climates such as tropical or arctic conditions; or wild camping in hostile weather conditions?

- **Decide when you will be camping**. Summer only, seasonal (spring and autumn), or all year?

- **Check the labels on a sleeping bag when purchasing**. They will tell you the insulation properties of the bag and what it is suitable for. Labels will read:

- o **One season**: suitable for summer only (in a British climate)
- o **Two season**: suitable for summer plus spring or autumn
- o **Three season**: suitable for everything except a really hard winter
- o **Four season**: suitable for all-year-round use
- o **Five season**: suitable for expedition use in arctic conditions or at high altitude

In general, the lighter and smaller the packed size, and the warmer the bag, the more you are likely to pay. Don't buy the cheapest regardless of how and where you're going to use the sleeping bag, but make your selection based on how you will use the bag the most. Think ahead if you believe you might need to upgrade later – spending a little more now on the right sleeping bag could save you money in the long run.

If space (ie you're not backpacking) is not a problem and you don't want to overheat in summer and freeze in winter, look to buy two sleeping bags for seasonal use – a lightweight mummy-shaped bag for summer that will fit into a larger, rectangular bag in cooler weather.

Sleeping bag liners

Look at buying a liner for your sleeping bag too. Cool cotton ones can be used like sheets in summer, and fleece liners can be used in autumn: both may save you needing to buy two sleeping bags as mentioned above. Either way, they will improve the bag's warmth significantly. As they are easily removed, they also have the added advantage of helping to keep the inside of your sleeping bag clean.

DUVETS

The alternative is to use your duvets from home to provide real comfort. Not so cocooned, they let your body breathe more than when you're in a sleeping bag. And, assuming you already possess them, it makes more economical sense to use what you've already got rather than buy extra bedding. They do take up a lot more space in your car though, so sleeping bags may be the answer if you're short of space on your travels.

Pocket Tip 🔥

White duvet covers and camping don't mix. If you want your duvet to look good enough to keep snuggling under, use darker-coloured duvet covers when camping.

✸ FOR CARRYING YOUR STUFF ✸

RUCKSACK

If you're backpacking on your camping trip, your rucksack is as important as the tent you sleep in. It could be on your back for much of the day and comfort is therefore of paramount importance; for your health as much as your enjoyment of camping in this way. Carrying everything that you need to camp is perfectly possible, providing that you're not expecting lots of luxuries, but you need to choose the right rucksack for the job – and the right rucksack for you.

Pocket Fact ⛺

The word 'rucksack' comes from the German words for back (Rücken) and bag (Sack).

Choosing a rucksack

When you're choosing a rucksack, think about size (according to your height and build) and fitness. How much you can carry comfortably is dependent upon this; as a general rule, one quarter of your bodyweight is the maximum you should try to carry.

Weight

Look at weight in terms of a bag of sugar: that is, 1kg. How many bags of sugar would you want to carry on your back for several hours – or days – at a time? It can be all too easy to keep piling in the objects (and weight) while you're packing the rucksack at home, but once you've done several miles with it on your back, with nowhere to lighten the load, it can feel even heavier. Do you really need all those items? What could you manage without?

Pocket Fact 🏕

In Britain rucksacks are measured in litres. You'll probably need a 65-litre rucksack to carry all your camping gear.

Comfort

The rucksack needs to sit on your back comfortably. The shoulder straps should be adjusted so that you are not stooping or feeling the weight heavy on your shoulders. The waist and/or hip straps should be positioned correctly and tightened to ensure that they are taking their share of the weight. If these two aspects are correct then the rucksack is at the right height. A framed rucksack will give you more support and better weight distribution than a frameless one.

Here are some essential points to keep in mind when choosing your backpack:

- The hips are stronger than the shoulders. Therefore, shoulder straps should merely be used to stabilise the load rather than carry it.

- Men and women carry a heavy load in different ways and need the weight distributed differently. Some manufacturers now sell gender-specific rucksacks. If you're likely to be using a rucksack frequently, carrying the load correctly is even more important to prevent back problems at a later date.

- Look at the construction and the materials used – is it rugged enough for your intended use? Check the waterproof qualities of the material and look to see if it includes a rain cover.

Pocket Tip 🔥

Look at the frame and back system. Does it have a mesh panel to increase airflow so it doesn't rub against you and create sweat?

Packing and carrying a rucksack

- Before packing, think about the order in which you need to *unpack* so that you don't need to pull the contents out all over the ground just to reach the item in the bottom. Your sleeping bag should be at the bottom as the last thing in the day that you need. Your waterproof coat should be at the top.

- Try to make sure that the pack is well balanced, with weight evenly distributed; the heaviest items should be closest to your back, in the middle of the rucksack.

- Make sure that items such as bedding and clothing are protected against rain, damp, and any liquids that you're carrying.

- Use outside pockets for items such as stoves and fuel, so that smells and leaks do not affect everything within the bag, and keep food separate from cooking fuel to prevent it from becoming tainted.

- Before you leave, and each day before you set off again, check that the straps are adjusted so that the rucksack feels comfortable, and always check that no hard objects are poking into your back. It always seems easier to repack while at a campsite rather than several miles along a hillside footpath.

Pocket Tip 🔥

If you're backpacking with friends or family and going to be sleeping in the same tent, share the load and pack separate tent parts so one person doesn't carry the burden. The same can be said for food and cooking equipment.

A rucksack checklist:

- Waterproof jacket and trousers

- Torch

- Tissues

- Sunscreen, sunglasses and sunhat

- Maps

- First aid kit

- Towel (try to get away with as small a towel as you possibly can to save space. Microfibre towels are handy: they have to be kept moist to work properly, so keep them in a sealed bag to avoid everything else getting damp)

- Water bottle (keep it easily accessible)

- Food including emergency sweets (Kendal Mint Cake is an obvious choice)

- Washing up liquid (you only need a tiny amount, and wrap it in a leak-proof bag)

- Stove and matches (make sure matches are not next to a liquid that could leak)

- Clothes and alternative, lightweight footwear to change into (you don't want to be in walking boots to head to the shower)

- Soap, toothbrush etc

- Cooking pan, cutlery, mug

- Sleeping mat

- Sleeping bag

- Tent

Keep travel documents such as confirmation of campsite bookings, passports, money, camera and other small personal belongings separate; these can be strapped to you using a money belt or something more secure than the back pocket of a rucksack.

Pocket Tip 🔥

Even more important than when packing a suitcase, use travel-sized bottles for shampoo and washing-up liquid.

DAYSACK

Unless your idea of camping is to not set foot out of the campsite until you leave to go home, a daysack may well be a requirement. They come in many different sizes ranging from 10 to 30 litres, so decide what you'll be using it for most before determining how big or small a daysack you'll need. These are some useful questions to ask yourself:

- Are you visiting a few tourist sites, and simply taking a camera, some money, and a cagoule?

- Are you hiking for the day?

- Are you taking a picnic (maybe for a whole family), or lunch and a bottle of water?

- Are you likely to be using it in wet or cold weather? (You may need room for extra clothes such as waterproof trousers or a fleece jacket.)

Pocket Tip 🔥

If you're using your daysack for a tourist day out, use one that has lots of pockets to hold sunglasses, car keys, tissues, sun protection, and money. However, beware the temptation to stuff it full of unnecessary items. Remember, you're only going out for the day!

Tiny Camper Tip 🖊

You can buy child-sized backpacks too, which children enjoy packing a few bits and bobs in. But be prepared for the fact that you might end up carrying it when they're tired and the novelty has worn off. Give them a limit on what to pack — there's no need to bring all five teddies!

⊛ FOR COOKING ⊛

You and your family may well want to eat more, not less, when out in the fresh air all day, every day, so having some decent cooking equipment is essential.

STOVES AND CAMPING KITCHENS

You can eat with your fingers if you forget cutlery, but you'll struggle to make anything hot without a stove or a pan. These, therefore, should be considered the most important items on the camper's list of cooking equipment.

The size of the stove and pan will be determined by the way you're going camping. A single-burner stove on the top of a small gas canister is all you're likely to want to carry around when back-packing, but it's going to take a long time to cook a family meal on one – and you'd be forever rushing to the camping shop to fill up on gas canisters too. A double-burner stove – or two single burners – should do well for a family, so think about how you will be camping, and who you will be camping with, before buying the first camping stove you see.

One of the easiest fuels to cook with when camping is gas, including LPG (liquid petroleum gas) in refillable containers. It's also the most obtainable on campsites and in camping shops. (See Chapter 5 for more on buying and using gas for camping.)

Pocket Tip 🔥

For your sake and your fellow campers, avoid petrol-fuelled stoves; the risk to your tent and your neighbours is just too great to be worth considering.

The alternative to a couple of stoves is to purchase a complete camping kitchen, which usually consists of a two or three-burner stove, a grill, and then some kind of preparation and storage area. Frankly this is only really justifiable if you go camping on a regular basis, ie several times a year, not just once a year for a weekend. A grill means that you can also make toast (and you won't realise how much you miss this staple until you can't make it either first thing in the morning or as a superb late night snack).

Some camping kitchens are getting really quite sophisticated, but for some campers this may go against the grain of what camping is really all about. Before buying, check how easy it is to set up and pack away or clean – and how stable it is. A simple stove on the ground might actually be safer than a snazzy kitchen on wonky legs.

Top five kitchen essentials v five kitchen luxuries

1. Single-burner stove	1. Barbecue
2. Whistling kettle	2. Electric toaster
3. Saucepan	3. Grill
4. Coolbox	4. Camping kitchen
5. Utensils	5. Camping fridge

PANS

You'll also need some pans to cook with. Again, decide who is camping and how you're going to camp. You really don't want to be carrying a cast iron pot in your rucksack if you're backpacking, but one small milk pan is not going to be sufficient to cook for a family.

You can buy special camping pans that are lightweight and use collapsible handles. If you buy these kinds of pans, check the sturdiness of the handle and that it won't actually collapse when cooking. Ideally, if you can afford the space and weight, take good, solid pans as you would use at home.

BARBECUES

A barbecue (see page 119 on cooking with barbecues) is an essential for some campers, with a choice of either gas-fired or conventional charcoal. You may have a preference for one or the other but consider the implications when camping – charcoal is inherently dirty for transportation and packed up against your sleeping equipment it's not ideal for transferring dirt or smells.

Gas on the other hand is cleaner and you'll almost certainly be able to replace empty canisters at campsite shops.

Using a barbecue is, obviously, really only in the domain of campers staying on a campsite, although you should always check that barbecues are allowed before firing one up. A backpacker is unlikely to wish to carry even an instant barbecue, and so should stick to more traditional methods of camping cooking.

✸ ELECTRICAL APPLIANCES ✸

A singing kettle on a primer stove is one of the iconic images of camping. However, if you're staying at a campsite with electric hook-ups – and you're going to stay on a pitch with one – you may wish to consider taking electric kitchen implements with you such as a kettle or toaster (see page 88 on how to use electric hook-ups at campsites).

Look to take low-wattage 'camping' items with you rather than the standard kettle from home, which is surprisingly thirsty on power and is likely to blow the fuse at the campsite, taking your supply – and anyone else's plugged into the same terminal – down. No campsite owner is going to be impressed if they are called out to fix the problem just as they sit down to their own dinner! Low wattage electric appliances such as kettles and toasters are available from many camping and caravanning shops.

✸ FRIDGES AND COOLBOXES ✸

There are campers who will take 'everything but the kitchen sink' quite literally, and that includes a full-size fridge. It's perhaps overkill and somewhat defeats the object of camping, but a family can get through more food when out in the fresh air than at home. And, however fresh it is, a lettuce will wilt pretty quickly when out in a hot sun; never mind chilling those canned drinks.

Again you need to think about who is going to be camping to determine the size of coolbox or fridge that you need. An insulated cool box should suffice for a couple and will provide enough room for milk, butter, cold drinks, and the ingredients for a couple of meals, but you'll struggle to keep enough food for a family of four in one. Don't forget to consider the room that will be taken up by the freezer blocks that will keep the food chilled. In fact, don't forget the freezer blocks at all!

Pocket Tip 🔥

Keep two sets of freezer blocks so that one can be freezing while the other is being used; most campsites provide a facility to freeze blocks. And label your blocks, keeping them in a bag together, to avoid confusion with others. They're less likely to 'go astray' that way.

If you'd like something a little more sophisticated, you can buy a coolbox with its own electric motor. They tend to run on 12V, so you can use it in the car while you're driving as well, meaning your drinks will be pre-chilled ready for your arrival at the campsite. Don't use the 12V socket in the car whilst you're at the campsite though or you'll find a flat battery when you next come to turn on the engine.

Camping fridges, also available from many of the larger camping stores, are another alternative, and the best idea if there are a few in the camping party. The finest are dual fuel, which run on electric if you stay on a campsite with a hook-up, or on bottled gas at other times.

Top five cooking utensils you can do without

1. Electric cupcake maker: cupcakes may be all the rage, but really. . .

2. Strawberry huller: just in case you're incapable of pulling the stalk from a strawberry.

3. Electronic (using batteries) wine breather: in case you don't open your bottle of wine in time for dinner.

4. Electric charcoal starter: for when you've run out of matches. Where are those batteries?

5. Electric marshmallow toaster: enough said!

✳ FOR EATING AT ✳

TABLES

You may feel that a table is not strictly necessary and it is perfectly possible (and good) to sit on the grass or in your tent to eat. However a table does transform family camping trips, not just for meal times but also for playing games. A table is also useful for preparing meals if you don't have a camping kitchen with an in-built preparation area.

There are so many different kinds of camping table to choose from, all folding in different ways to save space. You can get tables that fold in half, carrying a couple of stools too, tables where only the legs fold up, or a table with fold-up legs and a slatted roll-up top.

A camping table needs to be lightweight for travelling and easy to erect. However, rigidity is the most important factor even before weight. There's no point having a table set up, complete with candles lit and a deck of cards laid out if one flutter of wind knocks the whole lot over.

CHAIRS

Many outdoor chairs are becoming more luxurious nowadays. Full-size folding chairs are fine for sitting around outside the tent but, unless you have a large porch area with your tent, they can be next to useless inside. If space is strictly limited in the tent, think about taking a few cushions to sit on instead. They'll make the tent feel much cosier too. Alternatively, compact folding 'beach' chairs (essentially a padded cushion and back rest linked together with straps) are ideal for use in small tents with limited headroom.

Before you buy

Check the ease with which you can erect a table and chairs; some seem to be ridiculously complex for something that should be so simple.

Check the dimensions of the table and any chairs when folded, and make sure that they will fit into the car while still leaving space for other equipment.

Backpackers may wish to leave a table behind and rely on any tables provided at a campsite (some do provide the occasional picnic table), or an upturned log for a flat surface when camping wild.

⊛ FOR LIGHT ⊛

TORCHES

Some larger campsites have good lighting (sometimes it's actually intrusive), but every camper, whether in a tent, caravan or motorhome, needs a good reliable torch. It's essential for finding your way to the tent after an evening out, or for finding your way to the toilet in the night. A more powerful light to see what you're doing in and around your tent is good too.

Look for torches that use rechargeable batteries and think carefully before buying a ridiculously cheap torch; they're not all they are cracked up to be and rarely last very long before either the bulb needs replacing or the batteries go down.

If you use a torch with a high-powered light and beam, shine it mostly to the ground to walk while on the campsite rather than flashing it around. No camper appreciates having the bright light flicked in their eyes.

Head torches are great for camping. They leave your hands free to cook, do jobs and play games. Again though, look for models that have a directional beam so that, if you're sat together, you don't blind one another every time you move your head.

LANTERNS

Lanterns come in a large range of sizes and qualities. As with torches, don't necessarily buy the cheapest one available. It may have poor fuel economy and not be that powerful, making it irritating if you want to read or do anything that requires a stronger light source.

The most popular lanterns are powered by small disposable cartridges of liquid petroleum gas. Obviously all gas has its dangers, but used sensibly they have a good safety record.

You can also buy liquid fuel lanterns, using a fuel not dissimilar to petrol, though how many people would actually want to have one of these in their tent is debatable, when there are other much safer options.

Electric lanterns tend to be the safest, either run off rechargeable batteries or by their own rechargeable power packs. However, they tend not to give off as much light as a gas lantern.

With more and more campsites offering electric hook-ups, this is now a serious contender for lighting the tent. But just because you have a supply of electricity doesn't mean to say that you need to go mad on the lighting. Be sensible about how much light you actually need — in summer you may only need enough to get into bed. In autumn, as the nights draw in, you may need a light on for longer to read a book or cook a meal. A small fluorescent light gives the best kind of light for this.

Pocket Tip 🔥

At night-time, tent canvas is transparent when a light is shining through it from the inside. If you don't want other campers to see what you're doing inside your tent, don't put the light on!

Electric hook-ups

To plug into an electric hook-up on site, you'll need a dedicated electrical lead (not an ordinary domestic extension cable). On one end there will be a 230V site connector plug that is attached to the electric hook-up point. On the camper's tent end should be a purpose-made unit containing sockets for the appliances (see page 88 about using electric hook-ups at campsites).

Extension cables should be at least 25m in length so they can comfortably reach the nearest hook-up point.

These cables are not always sold in camping and outdoor shops, so if you're struggling to find one visit a caravan accessory store instead.

If possible, purchase an extension lead with an RCD (Residual Current Device) and an MCB (Miniature Circuit Breaker). An RCD is an indispensible safety measure that instantly cuts off the electricity if it detects an imbalance in the electric flow. The MCB prevents overload and will fuse if the load is greater than its rating.

Electrics abroad

Many of the electric hook-up connection boxes in Continental Europe use a different 3-pin plug and socket to the kind used in the UK. If you are going to use electric hook-ups in Europe you need a Euro hook-up adaptor that has a 230V UK site socket on one end and a Euro plug on the other. These are available from most camping and caravanning shops.

✤ FOR WEARING ✤

The difference between a good and bad camping trip can often be whether you feel comfortable and warm. It's all very well to assume that the sun will shine and the temperature will be warm every day just because you're going camping, but the reality can be quite different, and it's worth making sure that you have suitable clothing to dress appropriately. Don't just pack a pair of shorts and a t-shirt, thinking it will do. And if you're camping outside of the summer season, then the right clothing is even more essential.

CLOTHES

- Dressing for the outdoors means having layers. These layers trap air between them, which keep you warmer than one great big thick jumper. Layers also mean that you can add or take away clothing as the temperature changes.

- Firstly make sure that all your clothes include natural fibres or are made from the most modern man-made materials that allow your skin to breathe. Lightweight polyester fleeces, for example, tend to be better than thick and heavy pure wool jumpers. If the fleece gets wet it is not nearly as bulky or uncomfortable as pure wool, and it's likely to dry considerably quicker too.

- Have a base layer of leggings and a lightweight but long-sleeve shirt. Clothing that is termed as 'thermal insulated' works well here. Then add a pair of outdoor trousers that are water-repellent and a polar fleece jumper or jacket. Finally add a waterproof, breathable jacket and, if you're going hiking or walking in conditions that demand them, a pair of waterproof over-trousers or gaitors.

- Even when summer camping, it's worth packing a woolly hat (a sunhat is of course essential) and gloves. Hot summer days can turn surprisingly chilly at night and if you intend to sit outside chatting, the lack of movement will mean you feel the cold.

- A pair of bed socks, old-fashioned as they may be, is a godsend when you're cold at night. And for autumn camping, make sure you have some warm and cosy bed clothes to keep you feeling comfortable.

● You don't want to be traipsing around the campsite to the washrooms in your underwear or otherwise ready-dressed up to the nines, so find some comfortable clothing to slip on first thing in the morning to toddle off for a shower – a dressing gown, leggings or comfy trousers.

Thermal clothing

Clothing labels often advertise that they are 'thermal' or have thermal properties, but what does it mean? Think of a 'thermos' or vacuum flask. It is the air or vacuum between the layers that is keeping the contents warm, or cold if the contents are cold when they are put in. Thermal clothes work in a similar way: the more expensive 'thermal' clothing may use special fabrics and materials to regulate body temperature by allowing the skin to breathe (your body needs to release the humidity and sweat that heat produces).

For ordinary camping trips in an average British climate, expensive thermal products are not necessary – just stick to the rule of layers, using material that will allow your skin to breathe.

FOOTWEAR

Camping is all about comfort rather than style – although there is some very stylish camping gear out there now. Leave the high heels at home and stick with flat soles that will give you a good grip on potentially slippery and uneven ground.

Walking boots are the instant thought when camping; after all that's what all the camping and outdoor shops sell. However, you don't necessarily want a clod-hoppy lump of walking boot on your feet if you're simply staying on site for a family holiday in the sun. You can get much lighter-weight but still waterproof walking shoes – or sandals – that will do the trick. These will at least keep your feet warm and dry on colder evenings and wet weather days.

There's nothing quite like feeling soft grass beneath your feet on a warm summer day. But not all campsites are spotlessly clean or 100% grass, so take something with you to head across to the water tap, rubbish bins, or shop. Also take a pair of quick-drying, slip-on footwear, such as flip-flops or Crocs, for visiting washrooms and showers.

Pocket Tip 🏕

Take an old car mat or carpet samples (usually available from carpet shops for a few pence) to put at the front entrance of your tent. It will act as a reminder to take off footwear, rather than tread mud and grass all over your bedding.

FESTIVAL CLOTHING

As much as a backpacker heading off on an arctic expedition requires different clothing to the camper going on a beach holiday in the sun, festival campers need a few specialist things too (see Chapter 8 for more on festival camping).

It's accepted that festivals are as much about style as comfort, but you do need to remain comfortable if you want to have a good time. There's nothing like extremely sore blisters and wet feet to dampen the spirits of the party.

Wellies are great for the mud but they won't allow your feet to breathe if you're hanging around in them all day – and night. So take another breathable pair of shoes or boots too and use them as often as you can. And make sure that you wear socks with your wellies to prevent them from rubbing.

If style is of the utmost importance, look out for the trendy patterned wellies that you can now buy with wedge heels.

If you're going to wear walking boots and want to make sure that they remain waterproof while still allowing your feet to breathe (you do still want to feel comfortable after all), select a boot that has a lining that will do just that – like Gore-tex.

✦ CAMPING EXTRAS ✦

Sometimes having those little extras can make life so much easier at a campsite, especially if you're staying away from home for some time and you have the space to transport them.

- You may be the tidiest person in the world but your camping companions may not be. Some form of storage inside your tent will stop you from sleeping with children's toys at the bottom of your sleeping bag and dirty washing mixed up with your clean clothes. Take some soft collapsible boxes with you to help keep order.

- A flexible 'trug' bucket squashes down easily for packing into the car and you can use it for so many things: stand it on the wet floor in the shower room, bathe the baby in it for a quick strip wash, wash wellies, use it to play games, collect wood etc.

- A simple drying rack by the tent is perfect for drying tea towels, bath or swimming towels, socks and underwear. Hanging them from the guy ropes of the tent can cause irreparable damage to the tent.

- Take a small 'camping' tool kit with you, containing items such as spare ropes and spare pegs, glue, gaffer tape, cable ties, scissors, mallet, and patch kit.

- Your own chemical toilet and chemical tent can be useful if you're not that inclined to share the public facilities with others, and also if you find yourself on a pitch some distance from the amenity building. Perfect for those in-the-middle-of-the-night occasions!

- A portable solar shower is ideal if you're wild camping (they're lightweight and compact to carry) or if you're staying at camp-sites without facilities – though you'll need a shower tent as well to hide your modesty unless you're guaranteed to be alone.

Camping in luxury

For some, camping is all about getting back to basics and the call of the wild. For others, they won't set foot in a tent without a few added luxuries. Here are a few ideas:

- **Silk bed linen**. For that sensual feeling when you climb into bed.
- **Fairy lights**. Only use sets that are suitable for outdoor use.
- **Solar-powered garden lights**. Spiked, they can be pushed into the ground around your pitch, or at the very least at the ends of your guy ropes.
- **Kilim rugs**. Turn your tent into a boudoir spread with rugs.
- **Chimineas**. Check with the campsite before using one of these outdoor fireplaces, but you may get away with one if a barbecue is allowed.

⊛ INTERNET SHOPPING ⊛

How do you tell if what looks like a bargain in a picture really is such a good buy?

- If you're buying a tent that costs several hundred pounds off the internet, you really should go and see it first. Pictures can be deceptive and what looks like a good-sized tent for your needs may turn out to be tiny, even if the dimensions are included. Find a supplier that has a showroom or shop where you can see the tent (preferably erected) first before deciding to buy from an online supplier. If it's cheaper on the internet, mention this to the shop supplier – they may be able to match or better the price, saving you some time.

- Look at any conditions attached to a bargain: is it a returned, damaged item, shop-soiled, or an ex-demonstration model? Tents that are used in showrooms go through some real wear and tear with potential customers climbing in and out all season long, especially if they're used for an outdoor display, so check there are no existing flaws.

● Before throwing away one tent and buying a replacement because of missing or broken parts, check on websites such as eBay to see if you can find a similar second-hand tent to buy inexpensively. By putting the two together, you may come up with one good, useable tent.

● Never buy second-hand equipment that require fuels such as petrol, paraffin, gas, or other flammables. The consequences of faulty equipment are unthinkable.

⊛ MAKING CHECKLISTS ⊛

It's so easy to keep loading up the car or the rucksack with ever more equipment for what was going to be a simple weekend camping trip. Before you start packing, make an inventory of all the essentials that you will need for your trip (you can use the checklist at the back of this book to help you).

Pocket Tip 🔥

Tick off items as you load up and make these your priorities. If you can fit anything else in, consider it a bonus.

Equipment suppliers

These large suppliers have stores across the country as well as online outlets, so you can visit a store to check out a product and then perhaps take advantage of an online offer.

● **Go Outdoors**: *www.gooutdoors.co.uk*
● **Towsure**: *www.towsure.co.uk*
● **Yeomans Outdoor Leisure**: *www.yeomansoutdoors.co.uk*

3

CHOOSING WHERE TO CAMP

It can be a daunting business selecting the perfect spot to pitch up – if you placed your weary head at a different campsite every night for a lifetime, there would still be thousands that you'd never get to visit, and that's without stepping outside Europe. This chapter will help to guide you through the many types of campsites that are out there, and give advice on what to look for; from the size, to the number of facilities available, this will help you pick the best campsite for your trip.

✪ DIFFERENT TYPES OF CAMPSITES ✪

An initial approach to categorising campsites can be to simply pigeonhole them into three types purely by physical size and the number of pitches available. A campsite's size will often determine the facilities that are offered to campers and, in many cases, the ambience – although it's worth remembering that this is not always the case.

LARGE

Large campsites usually consist of over 100 pitches (campsites in Europe can have over 1,000 pitches). There are often lots of facilities, including on-site entertainment. Some may be described as a 'holiday centre' or a 'holiday park' and may include a mixture of mobile homes, ready-pitched tents, touring areas for caravans and motorhomes, as well as tent pitching areas. They can be very busy and noisy during the day and evening.

MEDIUM

A 'medium' sized campsite has between 30 and 100 pitches. Facilities can still be extensive, and include entertainment or the provisions to make your own entertainment – such as tennis courts, games rooms, or a swimming pool. They are sometimes described as a 'touring park', offering pitches for caravans, motorhomes, and tents. Some mobile homes may be on site.

SMALL

'Small' campsites will have up to 30 pitches (tiny sites only five or six) and facilities will be limited to personal health and hygiene. It is unlikely that there will be any provision for on-site entertainment.

Of course, there are exceptions to this. You may occasionally find a small campsite with an exceptional quantity of amenities open to campers, or a large campsite with limited amenities, relying on other factors such as its surroundings to draw in customers.

CERTIFICATED SITES

Planning laws in the UK (The Caravan Sites and Control of Development Act 1960) dictate that planning permission and a site licence issued by the local authority are required to operate a campsite. There are exceptions, however. Small campsites with a maximum of five units (caravan or motorhome) on site at any one time are permitted without planning permission provided that they are organised through an 'exempt organisation' as designated by the Act. Of most use to tent campers are Certificated Sites, which are operated by the Camping and Caravanning Club (see page 64) and accept tents and trailer tents. In order to use Certificated Sites lawfully, you must be a member of the Club.

The Caravan Club (see page 64) also operates Certificated Locations in a similar way, although these are only open to caravans and motorhomes; again, as members of the designated club.

Many of these sites are farmer's fields, small paddocks, pub car parks, or even gardens. Facilities will be very minimal – usually just a cold water tap, a rubbish bin, somewhere to empty chemical toilets, and possibly electric hook-up points. Occasionally you will find one with additional facilities such as a shower, toilets, the sale of farm produce, or even the use of a privately-owned swimming pool. What they lack in facilities though, they usually make up for in location and a low-key peaceful atmosphere.

SEASONAL SITES

Occasionally, you may come across a seasonal site that is open for just 28 days a year (the maximum time allowed to 'run' a campsite for tents without a licence), and solely for the use of tents, trailer tents, and folding caravans. Consequently they usually only operate during peak times (for example, in July and August), and can often be found in areas where there is a high volume of tourists such as Devon or Cornwall, as an unlimited number of tents is allowed on the site during those 28 days. You may therefore find it to be a large or a small site in terms of the number of pitches. As these are, quite legally, unlicensed sites (usually a farmer's field), there is unlikely to be any infrastructure or facilities, which can provide a liberating feeling. But you do therefore need to take everything with you – including a toilet (unless portable amenities are set up) and fresh water. Existing, licensed, campsites may also use additional fields as seasonal sites during busy peak periods where facilities will be available.

The first commercial campsite in Britain?

There is some evidence to suggest that a site in the Isle of Man was the first commercial campsite in Britain:

- *Date: Set up in 1894*
- *Location: Isle of Man*

- *Name: Cunningham's Camp*
- *Open: May and October for the summer season*

Only men were permitted at this early site but it proved very popular, with over 600 campers visiting every week.

✸ OTHER CAMPSITE CATEGORIES ✸

Although it's the quickest way, categorising a campsite by its size really is over-simplifying things, as there are so many other factors to take into consideration when finding a site that could turn your weekend into a dream or a nightmare. The following categories are very useful in identifying different types of campsite and are helpful when you are trying to decide if a particular campsite is right for you. See page 53 for more information on how to choose the best campsite for you.

- **Tents only**. Sites will have washing-up and kitchen facilities (but not necessarily cooking equipment). Ideal if you don't want to look at rows of caravans.

- **Tents and motorhomes/campervans only**. Some camp-sites are regulated to allow small campervans but not caravans on site.

- **Tents, motorhomes, and caravans accepted**. Will be a combination of a campsite and a touring park. The two areas are likely to be separated, making sure that there are grass pitches for tents.

- **Motorhomes and caravans only**. May not have any facilities on site as campers would be expected to use their own on-board equipment.

- **Adults only sites**. Not hedonistic hotbeds, but sites that are designed to provide peace and quiet for those who would pre-fer not to listen to the noise of children during their stay. Occasionally, some 'adults only' sites will allow grandchildren to visit during the daytime.

- **Family sites.** The larger holiday-park style sites work well if you require lots of activities and entertainment to keep the children amused. They are also best for meeting other children of a similar age.

- **Group friendly sites.** Some campsites will not accept groups at all. Others will accept two or three families who wish to camp together. Larger sites often provide a 'groups only' area. There are also campsites that will accept campers who are on Duke of Edinburgh Award expeditions.

- **Naturist sites.** Not necessarily 'adults only', many are family orientated. Most are run by naturist clubs for their members.

Pocket Fact 🏕

The Duke of Edinburgh Award is a programme of activities, including camping expeditions and charitable work, organised by a youth charity with the Duke of Edinburgh as its patron. The scheme comprises of Bronze, Silver and Gold awards and is open to anyone aged 14–25, regardless of their ability or background. See www.dofe.org for more details.

Using these categorisations, along with the size of the campsite, will help you to begin to wade through the vast numbers of those available to you and help you narrow down your choice.

Ready to go

Camping doesn't have to mean erecting a tent yourself; you can find a campsite where all the groundwork has been done for you. Simply turn up and chill out. And there are many ways to do this according to your preferences:

- *Fully-erected frame tents on large holiday parks with all of the amenities listed above.*
- *Yurts, tipis, camping pods, and safari-style tents in hidden locations, in woods and on farms.*

- *Caravans – either modern or retro in style – on conventional touring parks.*
- *Static caravans (or 'mobile' homes) on large holiday parks and smaller campsites.*
- *Hiring a motorhome or campervan – either modern or retro (such as a VW campervan).*

In all instances, beds and cooking facilities will be provided. It could be a campbed, a full four-poster bed if you're 'glamping' (see page 69), a hammock, or a futon. Cooking might include a small grill-oven, a barbecue, or a pan hung over a log fire.

✿ GRADING ✿

Most commercial campsites are graded on a scale of one to five, with various organisations providing the grading – including national tourist boards and the AA. However, these grades tend to be given according to the facilities that the campsite can offer rather than how stunning the location is or how warm the welcome can be. Therefore larger sites, with lots of facilities, are more likely to have a higher grading than a smaller site with limited facilities.

Pocket Tip 🔥

If you need a campsite with lots of facilities, check out the star rating. If atmosphere and location are more your scene, ignore a campsite's rating.

✿ FEATURES OF CAMPSITES ✿

The most common features that you will want and perhaps expect to look for at a campsite are:

- Showers
- Toilets
- Cooking facilities
- A shop selling basics such as bread and milk
- Play area

Obviously the number and quality of these features will depend on the size of the campsite, but generally you can expect that the larger the campsite, the bigger the number of different facilities.

In addition, these are some of the facilities that you are likely to find at a large, all-singing commercial campsite:

- Several amenity buildings with many showers and toilets, including disabled and family bathrooms, plus baby-changing facilities
- Washing-up and food preparation areas, including full kitchen areas with a cooker, microwave, fridge, and freezer
- Launderette and ironing board
- Large supermarket-style shops selling food, souvenirs, and camping accessories; they can also be licensed to sell alcohol
- Restaurant and bar
- Take-away food service
- Swimming pool(s) – indoor and out
- Playground
- Games room with facilities such as a TV, table tennis, pool, or billiards
- Sports facilities including tennis courts, cycle hire, watersports hire, fishing etc
- Private beach
- Family entertainment such as karaoke, pub quiz, talent shows, and childcare

- 24-hour check-in (mainly abroad, and particularly at city campsites), or long opening hours at reception

- Concierge service providing tickets and bookings for transport and tourist attractions

Medium-sized campsites may well have any of these facilities but on a lesser scale, while small-sized campsites are more inclined to have a combined shop (or none at all) and reception with limited opening hours, and minimal or no extra facilities.

✤ HOW TO FIND A CAMPSITE ✤

WORKING OUT YOUR IDEAL TYPE OF CAMPSITE

Before you begin searching for your ideal campsite (assuming you've already selected an area to visit), there are several questions you should ask yourself to help decide the ideal type of campsite for you:

- What do you want from your campsite? A secret hideaway with very few people, or a location that enables you to do a specific hobby?

- Who will you be travelling with? Are you meeting up with friends and camping as a group, or just as a couple?

- How long do you plan to stay – just one night while touring, a long weekend or a fortnight? The longer you stay, the more facilities you may require, such as a laundry or shop.

- Are you happiest with a simple farmer's field and a water tap, or do you require the full facilities of a five-star graded site with heated shower blocks, swimming pools, and entertainment provided?

- Are you camping with children (see Chapter 7) or would you prefer a site that caters only for adults, to ensure that a stray football doesn't hit your tent?

- Would you prefer a campsite where the tents are already erected and the barbecue is set up?

- Do you intend to cook your jacket potatoes over a smoulder-ing fire? If so, check that your chosen campsite will allow open fires.

- What kind of setting would you prefer – in the depths of a forest or within walking distance of the beach?

Make a note of your answers to these questions and make sure you keep them in mind when researching campsites. You need to keep your priorities in mind so you don't become distracted by the promise of amazing views but no laundry facilities – unless of course a stunning view is the most important aspect for you.

WHAT'S BEST FOR YOU?

Once you've figured out what you're looking for in a campsite, it's time to refer back to the types of categorisation mentioned earlier. Using these categories you will be able to figure out which type of campsite will best suit your needs.

- If you have a tent, look for a tent-only campsite, or ones that allow other forms of accommodation, according to what suits your needs/tastes best.

- If you have children, check the site isn't adults only and that there are the facilities you'll need to look after your children (perhaps toilets, showers, and entertainment).

- If you are taking a large group, especially if it's comprised mainly of children, check that the campsite allows groups and if there are any restrictions regarding noise.

- If you want to 'get away from it all', look for a very small site with limited facilities and just fresh air for company.

RESEARCHING CAMPSITES IN THE UK AND ABROAD

Now that you're aware of the type of campsite you're looking for, the easiest options for finding a campsite include the following.

Guidebooks

Good for regular campers who go camping several times a year, or for those touring who need details on lots of campsites. Thoroughly researched, they can often provide additional information about a campsite's location and attractions within the area.

A list of readily-available campsite guidebooks with target readership:

- *Cool Camping* series (covers England, Wales, Scotland, France, and Europe) – good for tents

- *Cool Caravanning* (covers England) – caravans and motorhomes

- *AA Caravan & Camping* series (covers Britain, Europe [in general], and France) – good for tents, caravans and motorhomes

- *Alan Rogers Guides* (covers countries throughout Europe) – good for tents, caravans and motorhomes

- *Time Out Camping: Our Favourite Sites in Britain* – good for tents

---

Thomas Holding and *The Camper's Handbook*

While camping for pleasure did exist before the turn of the 20th century, it was still only a marginal activity enjoyed by a select few. Thomas Hiram Holding is widely recognised as the man to change that. Holding is often called the founder of modern-day recreational camping and is credited with introducing camping to the masses.

Having taken adventurous trips across America as a child with his parents, Holding continued his love of outdoor pursuits as an adult, including cycling with his friends in the UK. He travelled to Ireland on a camping and cycling trip, chronicled in a book, Cycle and Camp in Connemara, *in which he requested other interested cyclists to get in touch.*

Along with these other cyclists, Holding formed the Association of Cycle Campers in 1901 with just 13 members.

> It has gone under various guises and amalgamated with other clubs over the years, and today it is known as the Camping and Caravanning Club.
>
> Keen to disseminate the information that he had accrued on his travels, Holding wrote The Camper's Handbook in 1908 to pass on his knowledge. It was the first book of instruction on camping.

Websites

Specialist websites with listings of campsites by geographical area can provide up-to-date reviews by other campers who have visited recently. Beware of old websites that have not been shut down, and which may have out-of-date information and reviews.

UK websites

- **www.ukcampsite.co.uk**. A comprehensive website that, despite its name, actually provides a search for both UK and French campsites. Searches can be made in geographic areas (by region, county, or town) or for campsites that will accept a certain type of camper (ie tents, caravans, or motorhomes), including campsites that only accept tents. Options can also be set to find specific requisites, such as campsites with sea views, fishing, open fires, a pub etc, and there are customer reviews and links to individual campsite websites.

- **www.caravansitefinder.co.uk**. A website covering the UK and Ireland mainly aimed at caravan and motorhome users, which includes plenty of campsite images and customer reviews. A geographic search can be made for region, county, or place name and there are also links to individual campsite websites.

European websites

There are very few campsite search websites in English covering continental Europe. Therefore, unless you have a good knowledge of the local language, the best places to look for European camp-sites on the internet are the official tourist information websites for each individual country. These however tend to only list the larger, graded campsites. Part of the fun of touring in Europe is to discover a tiny gem just around the corner, so ask your friends for recommendations or just set off on an adventure.

US and Canadian websites

The National Park Service (www.nps.gov) and National Recreation Reservation Service (www.recreation.gov) allow you to search for campgrounds within national parks and state-owned forests. These can be both state-owned and private campgrounds, and can include camping cabins and lodges, RV (recreational vehicle) touring parks, and minimal facility sites.

You can also search www.gocampingamerica.com, which lists over 3,700 private campgrounds and RV touring parks throughout the USA. All sites listed are members of The National Association of RV Parks and Campgrounds, with links to individual campsite websites.

Campgrounds in Canada can be searched for at www.camping-canada.com. The website provides an advanced search by location (province, region or city), campground type (privately-owned, municipal, provincial, or national), and additional features such as fishing, beaches, or pets allowed.

Websites for Australia and New Zealand

Australian campgrounds are listed under the accommodation sections of the Australian Tourist Board website: www.australia.com. Most are caravan parks that offer tent pitches.

New Zealand holiday parks (NZ campsites) are listed on the official tourist board website for the country: www.newzealand.com. Search under 'Accommodation' for a comprehensive listing giving information on location and facilities.

Back to nature 'Conservation Campsites' in New Zealand's national parks can be located on the Department of Conservation website: www.doc.govt.nz/parks-and-recreation/places-to-stay.

Magazines

Specialist camping magazines often provide reviews of campsites and ideas on places to stay for particular events and activities.

- *Camping* (www.campingmagazine.co.uk) is the only magazine specifically for tent campers. The magazine includes reviews of campsites and articles providing ideas on places to stay.

- *Practical Caravan* (www.practicalcaravan.com) and *Practical Motorhome* (www.practicalmotorhome.com) offer suggestions and reviews of campsites in every issue, both from seasoned travellers and novices.

Carry on Camping

Known to many for Barbara Windsor's bikini top landing on the face of Kenneth Williams, Carry on Camping *took to the movie screens in 1969 following a successful decade for the camping industry.*

The film follows the escapades of Sid and Bernie, who wish to take their chaste girlfriends to a nudist camp in the hope that they might 'lighten up'.

However, they soon discover that the dismal campsite they arrive at is not a naturist site after all and the tight-fisted owner will not provide a refund. Things go from bad to worse for the chaps when their girlfriends refuse to share a tent with them.

Chaos ensues with the arrival of a girls' finishing school led by Babs (Barbara Windsor) and Dr Soaper (Kenneth Williams) and other guests, including Peter, who hates camping but is put under the thumb by a domineering wife; Charlie the first-time camper; and a group of hippies arriving for an all-night rave.

Those new to camping may never set foot on a campsite if they believe all they see in this film, but it is a classic take on the joys of camping.

⊕ WHERE TO FIND CAMPSITES ⊕

IN THE UK

There are over 5,000 campsites throughout the British Isles, including tiny Certificated Sites and Locations. Many campsites are clustered in the most popular tourist areas, but you will always find a campsite within a few miles of any intended destination. Large holiday parks tend to be dotted around the coast, often in 'traditional' seaside resorts – the legacy of a bygone era.

> *Pocket Fact* 🏕
>
> *The most populated campsite areas of the UK are North and South Devon, Cornwall, the Peak District, and North Yorkshire.*

The future of camping looks bright and the 'staycation' seems here to stay. Campsites in the UK are reporting record bookings year-on-year and it's cool to holiday in Britain again. With an increase in airport tax, threats to transport systems worldwide and the average cost of a hotel holiday rising, a few square metres of the British countryside and some top quality local food on the barbecue is looking more appealing every day.

> *Pocket Fact* 🏕
>
> *In 2010, a camping holiday was more popular than staying at a bed and breakfast in Britain.*

IN EUROPE

France

France has one of the greatest numbers of campsites of any European country, with over 20,000 to select from. Again, these can be of any size and many are privately owned, although the country does have a large number of holiday-park style sites with pre-erected tents for those who don't have their own equipment.

However, France also has over 2,000 *Camping Municipal*, or 'Municipal Campsites'. These are run by the *mairie* (the town hall) and are sometimes linked to or found next to other leisure facilities within the town or village (such as a football pitch or sports club). They tend to offer excellent value for money as they are usually cheaper than privately-owned sites, and are often situated in stunning locations.

Small, farm campsites in France tend to come under two umbrella organisations: *Bienvenue à la Ferme* and *Camping à la Ferme* (a branch of the massive *Gîtes-de-France* organisation). These, again, are usually the most basic sites: simply a farmer's field with the most limited amenities – usually toilets and washing facilities, fresh water points, and maybe electric hook-ups. It is the umbrella organisations that the campsites are registered with (and inspected by); campers do not need to be members of the organisations to use the sites though.

Pocket Fact 🏕

The Vendée *is the* Département *(a little like counties in the UK) with the largest number of campsites in France.*

In other European countries

The Netherlands, Spain, Switzerland, Austria, Germany, Italy, and Scandinavian countries also have many campsites in varying degrees of size and quality. In Eastern Europe, there are fewer campsites and the quality of facilities does not always match up to the standards expected elsewhere.

Campsites in other European countries are not necessarily as vigorously regulated as the UK. Grading schemes may be different and the quality of facilities and pitches can vary enormously, so make sure you carry out thorough research rather than simply trusting a 5-star grading.

Pocket Fact 🏕

You can visit virtually every capital city in Europe by staying at a local campsite, as most capitals and major cities have at least one. They are often extremely large and very busy but they usually offer a welcome, leafy retreat from the bustling city streets. Many also sell tickets to nearby attractions. Check out the official tourist information website for the city concerned; there's usually a link to any local campsites.

IN THE USA AND CANADA

Campsites can be found all over the USA, with many located on state-owned ground such as national parks or Native American Reservations. These campsites can provide anything from the basics (virtually wild camping), to full-facility sites.

In Canada, there are both state-owned and privately-owned campsites. State-owned sites tend to be the cheapest while privately-owned sites offer more facilities. In both countries, hiring a motorhome (known as an RV, or recreational vehicle) is big business and many of the sites are geared towards the needs of these.

IN AUSTRALIA AND NEW ZEALAND

Most campgrounds in Australia are found in coastal areas and within national parks. Facilities range from very basic, no-facility campsites in extremely remote locations like bushland clearings, to caravan-only sites equivalent to a holiday park.

Likewise, New Zealand provides full-facility campsites (known as holiday parks) throughout the country, with swimming pools, barbecues, kitchen and dining facilities for tent campers and caravans for rent – but you can also find very basic, 'back to nature' campsites within national parks.

Pocket Fact 🏕

The town of Nelson, on the western tip of New Zealand's South Island, has the largest campsite in the whole of the southern hemisphere, with over 2,000 pitches.

⊛ HOW TO BOOK A CAMPSITE ⊛

Given how informal you'd expect camping to be by comparison to a more-than-luxurious top hotel, reading the 'How to' book information on some campsite websites can seem rather draconian. There can be lists of rules that request a monetary deposit to guarantee a booking, and concrete cancellation policies. This is usually because campsite owners have had their fingers burnt with campers who book and then don't bother to turn up, or wish to leave early without paying if the weather turns nasty. There is no single rule that covers every campsite, so double check on your right to cancel (ask them to send it via email/letter) when you make your booking.

Pocket Tip 🔥

Remember that, even if you are camping in a field, you are still obliged to abide by a business contract — just as if you were making a transaction in a shop or paying for a room in a hotel.

BOOKING PROTOCOL

- In the UK it's considered polite to pre-book (indeed it's almost essential during peak season) before arriving, even if it's a telephone call half an hour before arrival to check availability. You may find that the campsite sounds surprised if you want to book for just one night; many UK campsites have not yet got to grips with touring.

- In continental Europe, where touring is considered much more acceptable, you can simply turn up without booking in advance and arrive much later into the evening – up until 10pm during the summer.

- In Scandinavian countries (Denmark, Norway, Sweden and Finland), it's obligatory to purchase a *Camping Card Scandinavia* either online before you enter one of the countries (available from www.camping.dk [in Danish only], www.camping.no, www.camping.se, and www.camping.fi), at the border crossing, or at your first campsite before you pitch up. One card is valid for use in all four countries. It covers a named individual, their spouse or partner, and children, and is valid for 12 months. The card provides insurance while on campsites and offers discounts on equipment, services, and attractions.

- In the USA, many campgrounds within national parks and federal forests operate on a first come, first served basis. However, it may be necessary to purchase an entrance pass for certain parks. You can check which parks require permits at www.nps.gov (national parks), and www.fs.fed.us (forests).

- In New Zealand, it's advisable to book privately-owned holiday parks during peak season. Most basic 'Conservation Campsites' are operated on a first come, first served basis.

Pocket Tip 🔥

Some campsites, particularly in the UK, insist upon a minimum booking at peak times – such as Easter and bank holiday weekends.

BOOKING IN THE UK

- Decide the dates that you wish to stay.
- Check the campsite's own website for special offers.
- Use either the online booking service from the website, send an email requesting availability, or pick up the telephone. Most Certificated Sites and Certificated Locations (see page 46) are very informal and can only be booked by telephone.

- A deposit may be required, particularly for popular dates. This is either provided using a credit card or by sending a cheque.

- Make sure that you receive a booking confirmation and take this with you to show upon arrival at the campsite.

- Some campsites request payment in full upon arrival; others do not expect payment until the end of your stay.

Special offers and seasonal rates

Most campsites in the UK operate seasonal rates. As a rough guide:

- Low season is November to March.

- Mid season is April to June and September to October.

- Peak season is July and August plus Easter, May bank holidays, and sometimes the October half-term week. Campsites that are open all year will often consider the Christmas/New Year period as peak season too.

Campsites sometimes provide special offers such as three nights for the price of two, seven nights for the price of five, or discounts for OAPs, so make sure you check in case there are any offers you can take advantage of.

Pocket Tip ♨

If, for whatever reason, you need to cancel a booking, it is courteous to inform the campsite as soon as possible in order to free up the pitch for other customers.

BOOKING THROUGH THIRD PARTIES

There are no significant advantages to booking a campsite in the UK through a third party. Unlike hotels that issue a rack rate and then offer special, discounted rates through booking agencies, campsites usually stick to a single rate only.

Booking a campsite through a third party is useful however, if you wish to book a campsite abroad and struggle with the language. Bookings are generally made either through official tourist board websites, or through the booking centres of the major UK clubs (see below).

- Have as much information as you can about the site that you wish to book (name of site, address if possible), and the kind of pitch that you would like (ie for a tent, caravan, or motorhome etc).

- Also have the dates that you wish to book to hand.

- You may be asked for a deposit, or even the cost in full.

- Whether booking online or by telephone, ensure that you receive confirmation of your booking; it may only be a booking reference number. Take this with you to present upon arrival at the campsite.

Pocket Tip 🔥

Only make third party bookings, especially when supplying a deposit or credit card information, through official tourist boards and offices or reputable booking centres.

✴ CAMPING CLUBS AND DISCOUNT ✴ CAMPING CARDS

BELONGING TO A CLUB

The two biggest camping clubs in the UK are the Camping and Caravanning Club (www.campingandcaravanningclub.co.uk) and The Caravan Club (www.caravanclub.co.uk). Of the two, only the Camping and Caravanning Club is suitable for tent campers.

Both clubs operate a network of campsites, some of which are open to non-members (although club members pay a preferential nightly rate), while a few are for members only. The two organisations are also the umbrellas for thousands of small campsites known as Certificated Sites (Camping and Caravanning Club) and Certificated Locations (Caravan Club), which are only available to members of the respective club.

In addition, each club has a collection of regional associations that organise rallies both in the UK and abroad, as well as an annual national rally.

Other membership benefits include a booking service for ferry crossings and campsites in the UK and abroad, a monthly magazine, discounts on products and services, access to specialised insurance, and technical advice.

Pocket Fact 🏕

The Camping and Caravanning Club also has nine special interest clubs for a small additional fee, including: the Association of Lightweight Campers, for tent campers; the Canoe Camping Club, holding events for canoe enthusiasts; the Trailer Tent and Folding Camper Group; and the Mountain Activity Section, for campers who enjoy backpacking, caving, rambling, and pony-trekking.

CAMPING CARDS

Camping Card International (CCI)

The CCI is extremely useful when camping abroad, and is even considered obligatory in some countries and at certain campsites. It acts as a passport and a third-party insurance document throughout the world (insurance is exempt in the USA and Canada), eliminating the need for campsites to hold on to your passport (which they can do for insurance purposes should you damage any property). You must be a member of a club affiliated to an international camping association, which in the UK includes the Camping and Caravanning Club, the Caravan Club, the Motorcaravanners' Club, or the RAC to get a CCI.

Holders of the CCI also receive discounts at over 1,100 campsites throughout Europe. You can search for campsites that offer such discounts on the CCI website: (www.campingcardinternational.com).

Other discount cards

- **The ACSI Camping Card**. An annual card and associated campsite guidebook, offering discounts during the low season at 1,900 campsites throughout Europe. You can find out more at www.eurocampings.co.uk.

- **Camping Cheque**. Low season discounts: paying just one price at nearly 600 campsites across Europe. You order and pay for the 'cheques' in advance and simply hand them in to reception upon arrival. Check out www.campingcheque.co.uk.

⊛ WILD CAMPING ⊛

WHAT IS WILD CAMPING?

Camping anywhere other than in a designated campsite area is classed as 'wild camping'. It has alternative names in different countries; in New Zealand, for example, it's termed 'freedom camping'.

Where to wild camp

Wild camping should be just that – out in the wild, where there are no other accommodation options in the vicinity. It's not about pitching up in the entrance to a campsite (you're likely to get moved on quite quickly), or helping yourself to a farmer's field.

Minimal time

Common sense says that you should not stay at your wild 'campsite' for any more than a couple of nights, for two reasons:

- You'll attract undesirable creatures with your cooking and eating – whether it's rats in Britain or bears in Canada. So, for your own safety and health, move on.

- Wherever you're staying, the land belongs to someone and it's courteous to move on sooner rather than later, leaving the area exactly as you found it.

THE LAW

Finding places to wild camp legally both in the UK and abroad are few and far between. If you're adamant about wild camping as a hobby rather than a necessity, there are certain areas of the world that are better to head for than others.

In the UK

Wild camping in most parts of Britain is generally illegal, although there are a few exceptions. While CRoW (the Countryside Rights of Way Act) allows walking across certain areas of the countryside (see page 79), it does not provide the right to camp. Asking permission from the landowner *before* pitching a tent, whenever is practical, makes common sense – otherwise you could be prosecuted for trespassing.

Wild camping (in a tent or out in the open; not in a motorhome) is acceptable on parts of Dartmoor providing your pitch:

- Is for no more than two nights

- Is not on farmland (unless with permission)

- Is not on moorland that is enclosed by walls

- Is not within 100 metres of a road

- Is not on flood plains or archaeological sites

Pocket Tip 🔥

There are military firing ranges on Dartmoor, so take extra care when camping within a military zone. A map with suitable areas within Dartmoor National Park can be viewed at www.dartmoor-npa.gov.uk.

In Scotland, the Scottish Outdoor Access Code (2003) created the legal right to camp (see page 80). There are certain areas of land that are excluded from the Code, which can be viewed at www.outdooraccess-scotland.com.

In Europe

By far the best place to wild camp in Europe is Norway, Sweden, or Finland. They have a legal right to access land, including wild camping, known as the *allemenstretten*. In general, the rule is that wild camping is permitted in any open countryside (which excludes cultivated land), and must be done at least 150 metres away from the nearest house or cabin. In Finland, there are wild camping spots that provide a water supply (it may be a lake or river) and firewood.

In the USA and Canada

Wild camping is allowed in both countries, although the rules and regulations change from state to state. Many of the national parks and forests provide areas for wild camping where pitching a tent or sleeping overnight in an RV is perfectly legal.

Pocket Fact 🏕

Wild camping in the USA is known as boondocking.

In Australia and New Zealand

Both Australia and New Zealand accept wild camping, although the rules are likely to get tighter, particularly in New Zealand, in the light of irresponsible wild camping. Essentially, wild camping is only acceptable now for campers in motorhomes that have on-board toilets and waste water tanks. Campers without toilet facilities are asked to camp in designated campsites.

⊛ CAMPING FOR FREE ⊛

There are possibilities to stay on campsites free of charge, usually in return for volunteer work or some kind of help with basic jobs.

- **Seasonal fruit picking**. This can be done in the UK, particularly in fruit-growing areas around the Vale of Evesham and Kent. Abroad, there is fruit and grape-picking during the harvests of Europe, the USA, Australia, and New Zealand.

- **Helping on farms**. This could be a solution, especially if you have any rural skills to offer – clearing woodland, hedge-laying or planting, rebuilding stone walls, harvesting, etc.

- **As wardens or helpers on campsites**. Look for classified adverts in camping and caravanning magazines, particularly before the main camping season gets underway. Duties may include checking-in guests at reception, cleaning shower blocks, or mowing pitches.

Pocket Fact 🏕

You can also get free tickets (and camping) for some of the major music festivals, such as Glastonbury, in exchange for volunteer work like stewarding and litter picking. Check out the website for each event, but stewarding for Glastonbury is through www.oasiscarnival.co.uk.

✿ GLAMPING ✿

Camping has moved on from the somewhat downtrodden image it acquired in the 1970s. With new materials, tent derivatives, caravans, campervans and motorhomes all falling under the guise of 'camping', people have started to realise that camping can offer, to coin a phrase, 'something for everyone', and a resurgence in traditional camping, whatever that may be, is evident. Those who couldn't stomach life as a camper in the traditional way now find themselves drawn towards the 'traditional' tents of nomadic indigenous people and the cosy wooden camping pods now available on many campsites.

A cross between the most ancient and primitive forms of setting up camp and the package holiday of the 1970s has now arisen and we have a new word in the camping vocabulary: 'glamping', or glamorous camping. This new luxurious form of camping has taken Britain by storm and there are now a large number of sites offering accommodation in plush yurts, cosy tepees and a variety of other options which go beyond the traditional tent.

Pocket Tip 🔥

Check out websites such as www.goglamping.net and www.glamping-uk.co.uk to help you plan your luxurious stay in a yurt, tepee or converted Romany caravan.

4

HOW TO CAMP

'You put up a tent and you sleep in it' is the straightforward, trouble-free answer to the question of how to camp, but as with all things in life, there is a little bit more to it than that. Where you can put your tent up, where you can have a campfire, and how you deal with issues that might arise along the way (such as noise or hygiene), can make it a little more complex. But if you're armed with the knowledge, the 'how' of camping can be straightforward and fun.

✵ RULES, REGULATIONS, AND ✵ CAMPING ETIQUETTE

Rules and regulations are an inevitable part of life. There are countrywide legalities about where you can camp for example (see page 67), and then there are rules that are set out by campsite owners. These can often be found on a campsite's website, or the owner may provide you with a list of rules when you arrive. Sometimes, to be presented with a list of rules as soon as you arrive can appear a bit draconian, but campsite owners have usually had to draw up such rules because of the past behaviour or conduct of campers. You'll usually find that rules are there for your own safety and enjoyment, as well as for the safety and enjoyment of those around you.

Pocket Tip 🔥
Have a read-through of the rules as you may find that some of them actually form part of a contract on matters like cancellation of bookings, refunds upon leaving early, or damage to property, etc.

Make sure that everyone in your party is aware of any rules. On campsites with less paperwork, there may be just the odd sign posted that shows where to put the rubbish or when the reception is open. On the whole, whether there are pages of rules or just a few, it's best to use your common sense and follow them as best you can so that you have a safe and enjoyable experience.

DEALING WITH EMERGENCIES, PROBLEMS, AND COMPLAINTS

If you have a problem or a complaint to make at a campsite:

● Decide, is there an **emergency**? If yes, dial the emergency services (999 in the UK or, 112 in Europe) and then contact reception or the campsite owner. For all but the smallest of 'farmer's field' campsites, there is usually a noticeboard at the campsite providing an emergency out-of-hours contact number.

Pocket Fact 🏕

You can make an emergency call (to 999 or 112) on a mobile phone even if there is no signal and no credit registered.

● Is there a **problem**? Examples include an electric hook-up that won't work, a light bulb that's blown in the shower block or a noisy neighbour. If the reception is open, you can report the problem straight away. During out of hours, consider whether the problem requires instant attention or if it can wait until the reception opens again, either later in the day or the following morning. Campsite owners and managers are far more likely to be responsive and attentive if they are not woken in the middle of the night for a problem that could easily wait until morning to be rectified.

● Do you need to make a **complaint**? First, count to 10. Then ask yourself if the complaint is justified. If you feel it is, contact the reception during opening hours only and speak to the person managing the reception. This may be the campsite owner at smaller sites. If it isn't and you don't feel that your complaint has been handled effectively, ask to speak with the owner or manager.

Making complaints

Remember to remain calm at all times; you are likely to receive a much more favourable response than if you rant at the receptionist or the owner's son who is filling in to earn some pocket money. Many smaller campsites are family run – they may be a sideline to another business such as a farm – and as such are not set up to deal with formal complaints.

That said, you still have rights, and if you feel that your complaint is justified and has not been recognised then you can either:

- Vote with your feet and not return to the campsite again. If many customers turn away and business drops, the campsite will soon have to do something about it.

- Make a formal complaint, in writing, to the campsite and copy the letter to a relevant body – such as the head office of a membership organisation to which the campsite belongs, or the local council who awards a licence to the campsite. You must do this immediately though; a letter one month after a visit holds little weight.

PETS

The majority of campsites allow a dog. If a site indicates that dogs are welcome and you wish to take more than one dog, check first before arriving with a pack of hounds. Some sites may only accept one dog per unit (tent, caravan, motorhome) or pitch.

Other pets may be allowed at the discretion of the owner. Always check first before arriving with your pet alligator!

If a campsite does not accept pets of any kind, it is likely to be for a valid reason. Accept the decision and find another site if it's essential that you take your pet with you.

Even if pets are allowed on site, consider the behaviour of your pet and be considerate to fellow campers. Many sites accept 'well behaved dogs', for example. Nobody enjoys being kept awake by a dog that howls all night.

Some campsites will offer a designated dog walk or area to exercise pets. If this is provided, use it, rather than allowing your pet to foul the campsite grounds where people are pitching and playing.

Always clear up after your pet and dispose of any mess appropriately. There may be a dog bin on site. If there isn't, check with the owner before dumping it in any old receptacle.

You may find that pets are requested to be kept on a lead at all times while on the campsite, especially farm sites where there is a danger of your pet worrying farm animals.

Pocket Fact 🏕

Dogs and cats can carry a parasitic infection known as toxicariasis. It is carried in the faeces and can lie dormant in the ground where the faeces have been. Children playing in the same area can become infected, which can cause problems with fever, coughing, wheezing, skin rashes, and blindness. Therefore, you should never allow your pet to foul where children are likely to play.

THE NUMBER OF PEOPLE-PER-PITCH AND SPACING

There are no hard and fast rules as to how many people are allowed on a pitch, and it varies from campsite to campsite. Licences that are awarded to campsites by the local authority are usually for the number of pitches rather than the number of people, although there may be a limit applied to the number of people on a campsite at any one time for health and safety reasons.

Licensing the number of pitches usually regulates the number of people, as the campsite is likely to have their own rules on how many people per pitch they will allow. Check when you book if there is going to be a large number of people staying in one tent.

If you have a very large tent, caravan, or motorhome, you may be asked to take and pay for two pitches. This is assuming that the campsite can accommodate you, as not all have the space for large units.

Some campsites have strict rules on the spacing between pitches to aid fire safety. If they don't, and you're allowed to pitch any where you like, six metres is the general rule of thumb between you and the next unit. Besides, it's courteous not to pitch your tent almost on the top of your neighbours, especially if there is lots of space.

NOISE

Campsites, by their very nature, can be lively places, and no one wishes to be a party-pooper but campers have gone away for many differing reasons, and while one group may wish to party, another couple may have come for a quiet time. Some campsites are designated as 'adults only' so that they can advertise relaxation, peace, and quiet.

Some campsites are geared up for groups of people, such as young people carrying out Duke of Edinburgh Award tasks. Others may provide a section of the campsite specifically for groups where, for instance, two or three families wish to camp together. This is so that groups can be 'noisy' together without disturbing the remainder of the campsite.

If you wish to camp as a group, it is courteous to other campers to use these facilities. Explain to the campsite owner when you make a booking so that they can allocate a suitable area of the campsite for you. Likewise, if you're going specifically for some peace and quiet, it might be worth mentioning this when booking: the reception may be able to allocate you a suitable pitch. If you feel that having a group on site is going to cause you disturbance, then seek an alternative.

Many campsites will include a rule about noise after a certain time. However, be considerate to fellow campers at all other times too:

- Think about the use of radios and televisions during the day and evening; not everyone wishes to listen to the same station as you.

- Consider the use of 'white noise' items such as electronic games that bleep, or radio-controlled cars that can drive others to distraction.

- There's no need to enforce the archaic rule that 'children should be seen but not heard', but encourage children to be thoughtful about the noise they may be making while playing, and rein in unruly youngsters.

- Check that car alarms are unlikely to go off in the night – they sound much louder in a tent than through a double-glazed window.

- Be respectful of any campsite rules about noise after a certain time of night and keep chatter – and music – to a minimum. Remember that you may be having a party, but someone else may need a good, early night ready to get up and walk 20 miles the next day.

- Also be respectful of noise early in the morning. Those partygoers are sleeping it off as you rise early.

- Be considerate too if you arrive late at night (if you're allowed) or wish to leave early in the morning. Keep noise to an absolute minimum; think about hammering in tent pegs at 2am or discussing how to erect the tent in loud voices. Even zips can sound noisy if you're not having a good night's sleep. Don't slam car doors and drive slowly and quietly.

Pocket Tip 🔥

Some campsites in Europe – particularly in southern France, Spain, and Italy – have 'siesta' time during the afternoon, and you will be expected to keep noise to a minimum for a couple of hours. It may even be that you are not allowed to arrive or depart in a car during this time. Why not join them in an afternoon doze? It's bliss!

WHEN TO ARRIVE AND DEPART

Arrivals

If you have booked a pitch by email or over the phone, the campsite will usually provide you with arrival details with your confirmation (see page 63). If they haven't, make sure you call ahead to check if they have specified arrival times. Arrival times vary considerably between campsites and can be any time from 11am in the morning to 10pm at night. Most will usually provide a 'from' and 'to' time for check in.

If you think that you are likely to arrive early, don't assume that you can simply turn up. Some campsites have issues with narrow roads and entrances, and may need to stagger the arrival and departure times of guests to prevent clogging up the roads. Others may not have a vacated pitch prepared. A quick phone call to check should suffice.

Likewise, it is courteous to phone ahead if you think you may turn up after the allotted arrival time. Arrange your estimated time and try to stick to it if you can. It may be okay with large campsites that have a designated receptionist on duty, but at a tiny one-man-band campsite you may find the owner is desperately waiting for your arrival before they can go out.

Large, city campsites across Europe sometimes have 24-hour check in to accommodate backpackers arriving on late-night trains.

Smaller campsites that do not have a reception may operate a 'pitch-up' policy where you can find a pitch – a certain one may have already been allocated for you if you have booked ahead – and then sort out checking in and payment at a later time. The owner may come round once a day for example, or it may be that you settle up payment in the morning.

Pocket Fact 🏕

In Italy, campsites will ask for, and retain, your passport until you leave. This is their insurance against you should you damage any property. If you carry an Camping Card International (CCI) (see page 65), which includes third-party insurance while on campsites, then they shouldn't need to keep hold of your passport. They still might do so anyway!

Departures

Many campsites will operate a departure time by which you must have vacated your pitch and settled up your account. This is so they can do any maintenance (such as mow the grass), and have it ready for the next incumbent. It is usually in the morning between 10am and 12pm.

It may be possible to stay on longer if you want to, for example, make the most of a long weekend and not leave until Sunday afternoon. Check with the campsite *before* the requested departure time passes though. Some campsites will be very relaxed about it, particularly if they have plenty of space out of season. Others may request payment for an extra day, or simply cannot accommodate you if another guest is due on the pitch during busy periods.

If you wish to stay longer (ie further nights, rather than hours) than the amount of time you are booked, the sooner you ask, the more likely it is you'll be able to stay. But don't assume that you will be able to stay on the same pitch, as arriving guests may have specifically requested it.

Larger campsites may have a security barrier that is lowered overnight, and guests are asked not to drive on the site during that time. If this is likely to cause problems to an early departure, check the day before to make arrangements.

Pocket Tip 🔥

Some European campsites use locks on their electric hook-up points to prevent guests from fiddling with them. If you need to leave before the reception opens, bear this in mind, as you will require someone to unlock the box to retrieve your extension lead.

Remember to take away any rubbish or dispose of it properly. Take all of your belongings with you (even those chairs you don't want anymore), and leave the pitch as you would wish to find it.

PAYMENTS

Some campsites request full payment upon arrival. Others may take a deposit and ask you to settle up when you leave. If you need to leave by a certain time, allow for payments to be made. Large campsites can get very busy during checking out time and you may need to queue.

Pocket Tip 🔥

If the time by which you need to leave early in the morning is critical – to catch a ferry, for example – make sure that you have paid up the night before, so that you're not hanging around waiting for the reception to open.

Campsites may request a deposit for items such as entrance keys or cards to wash blocks (where showers, toilets, and washing-up facilities are located) and entrance barriers. The deposit will sometimes only be accepted in cash. Make sure that you have some with you if you want to get out and about.

✸ RULES OF THE COUNTRYSIDE AND ✸ RIGHTS OF WAY

Most campsites are of course in the countryside, and therefore consideration needs to be made for the environment you are staying in.

The Countryside Code is:

- Leave gates and property as you find them

- Protect plants and animals

- Take your litter home

- Keep dogs under close control

- Consider other people

- Be safe, plan ahead, and follow any signs

This code applies to England, Wales, and Northern Ireland. Scotland has a slightly different set of advice known as the **Scottish Outdoor Access Code.** It's quite similar, but includes advice on respecting landowners' privacy and taking responsibility for your own actions.

The code is merely advice for good practice in the countryside rather than law. However, you may find yourself in trouble with relevant laws if, for example, you were caught dropping litter, allowing your dog to worry sheep, or deliberately left a gate open to allow a field of cattle out onto a road.

Waymarkings

While out and about in the countryside be aware of how you are entitled to use public rights of way and how they are waymarked. The waymarkings are colour coded according to their use, and you'll find coloured markers along the route to advise you:

- **Footpaths**: yellow arrow – walkers only

- **Bridleways**: blue arrow – walkers, horseriders, and cyclists

- **Restricted Byways**: purple arrow – walkers, cyclists, horseriders and horse-drawn vehicles

- **Byways**: red arrow – all of the above, plus motor vehicles

The Countryside and Rights of Way (CRoW) Act was introduced into England, Wales, and Northern Ireland in 2000. It allows people to walk (ie not camping, cycling, etc) freely on ground known as open access land. This includes walking on mapped areas of mountain, moor, heath, downland, and registered common land, without having to stick to public paths. Similar legislation is governed in Scotland under the Land Reform (Scotland) Act 2003, providing unhindered access to open countryside. Coastal access around England is yet to be enforced under the Marine and Coast Access Act 2009 (which will provide the same kind of access as the CRoW Act), but the first stretches of the England Coast Path are due to open in 2011.

DOGS AND OPEN ACCESS

Some restrictions apply when walking on all open access land:

- From 1 March to 31 July, dogs must be kept on a short lead (no more than two metres) to protect ground-nesting birds.

- At all times of the year, dogs must be kept on a short lead (no more than two metres) in the vicinity of livestock.

Pocket Tip 🔥

You can check for up-to-date guidance on the implementation of rights of way and temporary restrictions at www.naturaleng-land.org.uk and www.outdooraccess-scotland.com.

✤ HAVING A CAMPFIRE ✤

Sitting by a campfire as dusk fades to darkness is one of the most exciting aspects of camping. Sadly it is rarely possible on campsites in the UK, with fears of safety and damage to property a major concern for owners. However, the trend to allow campfires is rising and it is beginning to get easier to find the odd one that will allow some form of fire.

When wild camping

- Firstly, check that you are allowed to light a fire where you are camping. Don't assume, if you are wild camping, that you can light a match wherever you like. There may be by-laws depending on where you are sited – such as close to forests, on heaths, or moorland – where the spread of fire could be extremely dangerous and damaging to the environment. If you can, check with the landowner first. Don't use, 'I didn't know' as an excuse for lighting a prohibited fire.

● You should never light a fire if you are in a very environmentally sensitive area, or if there is the remotest chance that you could set the countryside alight. If in doubt, don't light one.

● Neither should you light a fire if you need to chop down trees and branches to do so – they belong to someone! A fire will be very hard to light (and keep going) with green wood anyway, so only light a fire if there is sufficient dead wood that you can collect off the ground. And remember to reinstate the site of the fire back to the way it was (as best you can) before you leave.

At a campsite

● As with wild camping, check before you light a fire that it is allowed. Do this when you make the campsite booking if it is a major contributing factor to your camping trip.

● Those campsites that do allow them will have strict rules on lighting fires, for everyone's safety and for the environment of the campsite. It is rare, for example, to be allowed to light a campfire wherever you feel like it. There will almost certainly be designated campfire pits for small, individual fires, or sometimes large communal bonfires.

● Some campsites will insist upon the fire being kept off the ground, and so they will usually provide either a brazier or other device to keep the grass in as good a condition as possible. Wood will almost certainly be provided by the campsite, to stop guests chopping down the surrounding trees; you will usually pay an additional charge for the wood and some fire-lighting equipment, and, in some instances, you are not allowed to supply your own (campsites are in business after all!).

● Light your fire well away from your tent and those of others. And remember that, like barbecues, your neighbours don't particularly want to be smoked out, or find their washing covered in ash. Be considerate and take care while the fire is lit.

HOW TO LIGHT A FIRE

It may be that you need to rub two sticks together under emergency survival situations, but those that have thought ahead will take a firelighter with them on their camping trip. Keeping a cigarette lighter in your camping kit is useful too, rather than finding that your matches are damp and won't strike.

Pocket Fact 🏕

'Lifeboat matches' have a waterproof coating that allows the match to strike in almost all weathers, including strong winds and heavy rain. You're unlikely to even contemplate sitting around a campfire at a campsite if the weather is this inclement, but it's worth taking lifeboat matches if you're backpacking — making sure that you keep them in a waterproof container. Lifeboat matches are considerably more expensive than ordinary matches so they're not good for everyday use!

Easy steps for lighting a fire

1. Collect your wood before lighting the fire. Have some small, tinder like dry (if possible) twigs for starting the fire, and a selection of logs up to arm-width size. Make sure it's all within easy reach before you start trying to light the fire.

2. If you can, look for certain kinds of wood – ash is one of the best slow burners. Resinous woods such as pine will burn well, and dry hawthorn twigs (watch for spikes) are very good for getting a fire going. Willow, if it is dry, burns well but is inclined to 'spit' – so watch for sparks.

3. Choose bare ground well away from your tent, equipment, and vegetation such as hedges or crops. Use an existing fire pit if there is one rather than creating a new one (providing it is in a safe place). Consider the prevailing wind direction – you

don't want a tent filled with smoke because you've created your fire in the wrong place.

4. If there is only grass, dig a small hole – removing the turf carefully so that it can be put back in place when you move on.

5. Set your firelighter in the centre of your fire pit. If you do not have a firelighter, use things such as pine cones, pine needles, and dry leaves. Set it alight then add the tiniest twigs first. As these twigs get established add more, slightly larger twigs, and so on. Do not add larger wood too quickly or you will kill the fire.

6. When you have finished with your fire (and it is completely cold), spread out the ash so that it is unobtrusive and replace any turf that you have removed. Never leave with the fire still smouldering – it could reignite.

Pocket Tip 🔥

Be vigilant at all times, and be extremely considerate of the environment and climatic conditions. You do not want to be responsible for burning an entire heathland, a farmer's barn full of straw, or worse, people and their homes. Have a bucket of water close by before you light your fire.

When fires get out of control

- All licensed campsites are expected to have some form of fire-fighting equipment. It may be a bucket of sand (ready) or extinguishers.

- If the fire is small, you may be able to beat it out or pour water on it; when wild camping you may be able to smother it with soil (campsite owners won't be best pleased if you begin digging up their turf).

- If the fire is out of control, evacuate the area and make sure that all other campers do so too, before dialling 999 as soon as possible.

⊛ USING GAS ⊛

Gas – or liquid petroleum gas (LPG), to give it its full name – is used to fuel most camping stoves, barbecues, lanterns and any other appliance when not being powered by electricity. It comes in many brand names – Calor being one of the best known – and is easy to purchase throughout the UK. However, you cannot purchase Calor anywhere abroad. The most internationally-recognised brand is Campingaz.

GAS BOTTLES

Many gas bottles are returnable; you pay a deposit on your initial bottle and then as and when you swap it, you are (in theory) then just paying for the gas that is inside the bottle. Providing it is the same brand name, you can swap bottles anywhere; it does not have to be where you bought the first bottle.

There are two types of LPG used mostly in camping: **butane** and **propane**. Butane is the most common and is fine for summer camping in the UK, but it does not work (as it vaporises) at temperatures below 2°C. Propane is required for camping in other seasons, or when camping abroad in cooler climates. However, it needs to be stored at a much higher pressure than butane and is therefore placed in stronger containers, which are often heavier – something to consider if weight is an issue when travelling.

Pocket Fact 🏕

In the UK, butane comes in blue bottles and propane uses red bottles. Butane is not available in Scandinavia owing to the lower climatic temperatures.

Both types of LPG require their own regulator that fits onto the top of the gas bottle, which is connected to a piece of hose that in turn connects to your appliance. A butane regulator will not fit on a propane bottle and vice versa, but you need to check when purchasing that it will match your bottle.

What size bottle?

There are numerous sizes of bottles, all of which are measured in weight (the amount of gas in the bottle, not the overall weight including the bottle). This will vary depending on the brand, but average-sized bottles are:

- *Butane: 2.7kg, 4.5kg, 13kg, 15kg*
- *Propane: 3.9kg, 11kg, 13kg*

What size you need really depends on the appliance that it is expected to run — you may require a larger bottle for a barbecue, for example, but a small lantern will use a small canister rather than a bottle with a regulator. Of course, it's generally cheaper by ratio the more gas that you buy. However, few campers (except caravan and motorhome users) will require the larger-sized bottle unless you're going to stay on site for several weeks.

Many larger campsites sell gas but these are likely to be the smaller bottles (4.5kg butane or 3.9kg propane or less) and usually it will be a national or internationally-recognised brand. Many petrol stations will also supply gas in bottles and in tanks for refillable bottles (see below).

Gas bottles are, for safety reasons as described above, quite heavy. Light alternatives are available, such as BP Gas Light, though these are not so widely distributed.

You can also buy refillable gas bottles, which are very useful in that you can top them up at your convenience from LPG tanks (usually at petrol filling stations). It also means that you never waste any gas; a common problem for campers who never quite finish the contents of a bottle but need to change it in order to give them a full supply next time — running out of gas part way through cooking on the barbecue (guaranteed to happen at a time when you can't instantly purchase some more) is more than an irritation.

DISPOSABLE GAS CARTRIDGES

One other way that LPG – both butane and propane – is supplied is in disposable cartridges (Campingaz is the most well known brand here). They come in several shapes and sizes and in two formats:

- A pierceable cartridge that is fitted to your appliance using a hollow spike, which lets out the gas. Once the gas canister has been pierced it must remain fitted to the appliance until the gas has run out.

- A cartridge that comes with its own integral valve that can be removed from the appliance when travelling. The valve then seals the unit again. These usually have a screw fitting.

Pocket Tip 🔥

When you buy gas appliances, make sure that you can use a universally-available gas rather than the manufacturer's own. The fittings may be different and you could be stuck with a system for which you cannot readily buy gas refills.

How to use gas

- Make sure that you're familiar with the way a gas cartridge fits on the appliance, or the regulator fits onto the gas bottle. Instructions should come with any gas-powered appliance.

- Check that the appliance is switched off before fitting a new cartridge.

- Never change the canister or bottle inside your tent or inside a building – do it outside and make sure that there are no naked flames close by that might ignite any leaks.

- If you think that an appliance is leaking, get everyone away from it until the container is empty and the gas has dispersed naturally.

- Dispose of empty gas cartridges with care. Never throw them on a fire as any gas residue could lead to an explosion.

- Don't move appliances that are connected to gas while they are switched on. The gas needs to remain settled to be safe.

- Always keep gas bottles and canisters upright, even when travelling.

⊛ USING ELECTRIC HOOK-UPS ⊛

Once the mainstay for caravan and motorhome pitches, more and more campsites are now offering electric hook-ups on tent pitches. During the summer they can help to run a coolbox or a fan, but even if you don't use a hook-up throughout the summer months, having electricity on site is certainly worth thinking about for those planning some autumn camping when lights are likely to be on for longer. (See page 38 for the equipment that you will need in order to use hook-ups on campsites.)

You can use electric hook-ups for powering your coolbox, inflating mattresses, the mobile phone charger, laptop use (for music or watching the occasional DVD on wet nights), and a low-wattage electric kettle or toaster.

Electric hook-up points usually come in clusters dotted around the campsite, where anything from two to eight sockets are available; one per pitch. They may be numbered to correspond with a pitch number or it may be up to you to plug into an empty socket.

With most sockets you simply push the plug on the end of your extension lead (see page 38) into the socket and away you go. Some may require you to twist the plug in the socket in order to turn the connection on; others may require you to flick a switch. Ask the campsite manager if you're not sure.

Hints and tips on using electrics on campsites:

- Don't use too many appliances at the same time.

- Only use one appliance per socket; never use a multi-plug adaptor on campsites or you will overload the network.

- Switch off electric appliances if the inside of your tent gets wet.

- Keep sockets clear of the ground.

- Keep your extension cable well maintained and check for any nicks on the plastic sheath.

- Don't coil a mains lead too tightly when in use as it may overheat.

- Don't leave appliances switched on and plugged in when away from the tent. And never use beauty products such as hair curlers/straighteners that could be left on bedding; save those for use in the amenity building.

- If you don't use hook-ups (or there aren't any on site), use a power inverter to charge mobile phones, camera batteries, iPods, and torches from your car battery.

- Never touch any connections within the hook-up terminal other than when plugging in. If there is a problem, check with the campsite.

- Never unplug someone else's extension cable in order to plug yours in; it is considered extremely bad manners!

✤ DEALING WITH THE WEATHER ✤

Fair weather camping is wonderful but it doesn't always go according to plan, particularly with the predictably unpredictable British weather.

SUNSHINE AND HEAT

It's easy to forget the effects of both sun and heat when you're sitting around chatting, having a drink, and generally enjoying yourself on the campsite. But you need to take heat stroke and sunburn seriously, and a little forethought before beginning your daily activities will help.

Your skin needs to be able to breathe and sweat to prevent it from overheating. You are therefore most likely to suffer in humid conditions when sweat can't evaporate to cool you down.

There are two stages to overheating: heat exhaustion followed by heat stroke.

Heat exhaustion

Symptoms:

- You feel sick and giddy and your skin is sweaty, but you may feel cold.

- You may also feel excessively tired.

Avoidance:

- Wear clothes appropriate for the day and don't wear too many layers.

- Rest during the hottest part of the day.

- Drink plenty of water (more than you would on a 'normal' day) and avoid excessive alcohol.

- Wear a hat, and if you're out and about, take your activities gently.

Treatment:

- Sip water or a sports drink that has electrolytes in it for rehydration.

- Lie somewhere cool and shady.

Tiny Camper Tip 🖋

Small children and babies find it much harder to regulate their body temperature (and are much more likely to be doing lots of running around at a campsite). Encourage them to have 'cooling off' periods every few minutes in between running about, and find something quiet and relaxing to do out of the sun during the hottest part of the day.

Heat stroke

Symptoms:

- Your skin is dry, pink and warm.

- You feel unbearably hot, you can become delirious, and you may faint.

Avoidance: As for heat exhaustion.

Treatment:

- Heat stroke is far more serious than heat exhaustion. It can be fatal as it means your body's temperature regulating system is breaking down. You need external cooling by lying wrapped in sheets wet with cool (but not ice cold) water.

- Keep the sheets wet. However, you must be extremely careful about fainting while in water – do not go into water when suffering from heat stroke.

- Get medical help fast.

Pocket Fact 🏕

'Shallow water blackout' is a faint underwater, and despite its name it can happen at any depth. If you faint on the ground, your body rushes oxygen to your head and you gradually come round. When you faint in water, your lungs fill up – causing you to drown. If someone faints in water, every second counts and they must be extracted immediately.

Sunburn

It can take just 10 minutes to burn in full sun, even in Britain. Campsites can often be very open with little shade for respite, so look for a shady area (even if it's within the shade of a hedge) or go indoors during the hottest part of the day (usually between 11am and 3pm).

Symptoms:

- Your skin is pink then red, and blisters or flakes off.

- It is dry and feels very sore and hot to touch.

Avoidance:

- Keep your skin covered (cool, crisp cottons in pale colours are best) and wear a hat.

- Apply a sun cream and don't forget your face.

Treatment:

- Treat mild sunburn with cold compresses of water. Aloe-based products are also soothing.

- Drink plenty of water to remain hydrated and keep out of the sun until fully recovered.

Remember that sea breezes along the coast can be deceptive, making you feel relatively cool while being unaware that your skin is burning. Keep applying the sun cream and cover up when you can.

Pocket Fact 🏕

The SPF number (or Sun Protection Factor) given on bottles of sun cream loosely indicates the amount of time you can be exposed without getting burnt, relative to the amount of time without the sunscreen. In other words, if you apply an SPF of 20, your skin should not burn until it has been exposed to 20 times the amount of sunshine that it would normally take for you to burn without any protection.

HEAVY RAIN AND WIND

A light shower while you're tucked up cosily in your tent can be a really pleasant experience. However, camping in severe rainstorms is not fun when you're paddling about in muddy conditions.

Keeping yourself and others warm and dry is more important than keeping the tent or any camping equipment from spoiling.

If the weather is deteriorating fast and there is a likelihood of severe flooding, keep in touch with the campsite reception. It may be that they request you to move to higher ground or, indeed, that it is necessary to close the campsite altogether.

If a heavy rainstorm is expected in the night, get as much equipment as you can under cover, unplug and remove any electrical items, and place them somewhere that will remain dry.

Your safety is paramount. It might not be that comfortable, but shelter in a car rather than a tent that is going to be flooded or swept away in a strong gust of wind. Don't attempt to pack the tent up in strong winds.

Remaining in wet clothes, particularly when the weather is cold, is when hypothermia can set in, so keep your clothes dry by wearing a waterproof jacket and trousers.

Lightning

Lightning is a discharge of electrical current that is trying to find the quickest route to earth through the use of conductors. It therefore 'searches' for high points through which to channel.

If you're on a campsite, and there is the availability of shelter indoors, it's simple really – head inside and stay there until the storm has passed.

If, however, you're stuck outdoors with nowhere to shelter, get down to somewhere safe (the top of a mountain is not ideal), make sure that you are not carrying any metal, and, if you are, put it to one side and stay well away from it. Lie flat on the ground or crouch down to make sure that you are not the tallest thing in the area, and try to get some insulation between you and the ground such as rubber soled boots or a folded blanket (not a foil emergency blanket).

Safe places to shelter during a lightning strike are:

- Indoors, away from metal pipes
- In a car or shelter, such as a barn or shepherd's hut
- Inside a cave
- On the valley floor
- Among the lowest of anything – including trees or rocks, where there are higher ones close by

Dangerous places:

- Tents with metal poles
- High ground

- Under an isolated tree

- Under an umbrella

- Close to large metal objects

- Any place where you are the highest object

- The tops of towers

Pocket Fact 🏕

As soon as you have seen lightning, start counting the seconds before you hear thunder. Ten seconds means the storm is two miles away.

SNOW AND HAIL

Snow is an insulator and can keep you surprisingly warm. However, if you are caught in a snow blizzard or hail storm while walking, it can cause snow 'blindness' and disorientation.

Most modern materials used for standard summer camping tents will repel a certain amount of snow, but in a heavy snow storm the weight of lying snow will cause the fly sheet of a tent to sag, the poles to buckle, and the tent to collapse. Tents manufactured for arctic conditions are designed much more rigorously to withstand blizzards and high winds.

If you should get caught in a blizzard while out walking:

- Try to find shelter as soon as possible as the cold can cause hypothermia. However, you should also be aware of your surroundings, such as drops off hillsides, the moment that you became 'blinded' by the storm.

- Only move to shelter if you know that it is close by and can see far enough ahead to reach it.

- Try to remain dry and keep your hands, head, and ears covered.

- If you have the means with you, call for help and try to provide some idea of your bearings.

- Keep your body moving very gently on the spot to prevent hypothermia (no excessive exercise is required as this can put additional strain on your body in cold weather).

SEASONAL CAMPING

With the improvement in the technology of fabrics for tents and clothing, it is now easier to enjoy camping outside of the traditional summer season. More and more campsites in the UK are staying open throughout the year, and implementing cold weather facilities such as under-floor heating in amenity blocks.

To extend the season:

- Head for a campsite that allows campfires in autumn and winter, to brighten and warm the dark evenings.

- Find a site that includes an indoor games room or lounge area where you can get inside if it's really wet or cold – although check that bars and restaurants will be open, as many campsites reduce their facilities in the autumn and winter months.

- Look for a site that has heating in toilet and shower areas, with plenty of hot water. Cold showers are for summer only!

- Be prepared for wet weather by packing wellies and warm waterproof coats and trousers for both children and adults.

- Take plenty of indoor entertainment such as card games, dominoes, and good books rather than all the outdoor gear. Although something lightweight and not too bulky – such as a Frisbee – is a great thing to have for dashing around to warm up.

In bed:

- Pack additional blankets and extra batteries/gas canisters for torches and lanterns.

- Think about adding a fleece liner to your sleeping bag, which will give you extra warmth and comfort for cold camping but can be taken out during the summer.

- Put a hot water bottle inside your sleeping bag or bedding half an hour before you want to go to bed on chilly nights and your bed will be toasty warm when you get in. Or, if you don't want to mess about with hot water bottles, try using an instant hand warmer instead.

- Add extra layers: wrap up with a fleece blanket through the night and tuck a duvet around your sleeping bag – or sleep in a bag tucked inside another sleeping bag. Also add a fleece blanket, mattress topper, duvet, or picnic rug beneath your sleeping bag and on top of your sleeping mat/airbed.

- Cuddling up together with your partner in one sleeping bag will help with added warmth. Zip two sleeping bags together to create a larger 'double' bag, or buy a double-sized sleeping bag.

- Sleeping bags will lose their insulation value when damp, so try not to sleep with your head under the covers breathing out moisture. If your sleeping bag or bedding does get damp overnight, try to air it in any sunshine and wind the following day.

- Unpack your bag as early as possible if the weather is dry. Sleeping bags that have been crammed into sacks or backpacks need a while to recover their loft and insulating properties.

- You don't need to look like Wee Willie Winkie, but it's worth wearing a hat in bed if it's really cold as it's the head where most heat is lost.

- It goes without saying really, but eating well and eating the right kinds of foods – hearty stews, soups and other nourishing hot meals – will help to keep you warm throughout the night.

✾ HEALTH AND TOILET ISSUES ✾

Staying healthy during your camping trip makes it very enjoyable. Feeling ill can seem much worse when you don't have the comforts of home around you.

STAYING HEALTHY

Being outdoors, maybe staying at farm campsites where animals are around, can bring you much more into contact with different kinds of bacteria. There's no need to be obsessive about hand-washing, but use common sense and make sure hands are washed after using public toilets on campsites, having handled or stroked animals (or even opening gates on walks where livestock have been), and before preparing food.

Pocket Tip 🔥

Antibacterial hand gel is great for campsites as well as back-packing, picnics and walks.

Many campsites have luxurious amenity facilities that are spotlessly maintained, with eco-friendly shower rooms and plenty of space for washing and preening. If, however, there are no showers – or you just don't like the look of them – you can always have a strip wash using the washbasin and a flannel. But do leave the place clean and tidy afterwards, not flooded with water!

You might deem it necessary to smother yourself in lashings of *eau de toilette* to cover up a lack of washing for a weekend, but remember that perfume and aftershave can attract mosquitoes.

Pocket Tip 🔥

Wet wipes and absorbent kitchen towels are very useful on camp-sites, particularly when camping with children, but the anti-bacterial versions are also great for cleaning surfaces.

TOILET ISSUES

Motorhome and caravan users are fortunate to have their own toilet facilities on board most of the time. But for tent campers, the quality of the toilets and showers can determine whether you want to return to a campsite ever again. Most campsites do provide a toilet if tents are allowed on site, but don't assume this will be the case. If the information about a site doesn't mention toilet facilities it would be worth checking what is available.

Some toilets and shower areas can appear pretty dreadful, but it's not all down to the campsite staff to keep things clean. Treat the area as you would wish to find it and, if everyone else does the same, it will be much more pleasant for all. Encourage children to treat the facilities with respect too: you wouldn't allow them to flood your bathroom and you wouldn't throw toilet paper on the floor at home. Some campsites do have a rule that young children must be accompanied to use the facilities. It's for their safety and everyone's benefit.

DO NOT, under any circumstances, urinate straight out of the tent because you don't wish to walk to the toilet block in the night. It's downright disgusting, unhygienic, you could have children playing in the very same spot the following morning or you, or fellow campers, could be eating breakfast there too. You'll find the smell pretty unpleasant too.

Pocket Tip 🔥

Remember to pack a spare toilet roll. Campsite facilities can get very busy at 'peak times' and there are not always a sufficient number of toilets for campers, meaning that the cleaners may not have replenished toilet roll supplies before you get caught short! Of course, the toilet roll that's supplied is not always the most luxurious either . . .

Portable toilets

If you prefer the use of your own toilet to the public toilets, a portable loo and toilet tent on your pitch is a solution. A chemical loo is effectively a temporary toilet with a cassette beneath the seat and pan that holds the contents until you are able to empty it in a designated chemical WC disposal area. Portable toilets come in various sizes according to their capacity (usually measured in litres). Unless you want to be constantly emptying the cassette, select a larger capacity model when a family are likely to be using the toilet.

How to use a portable 'chemical' toilet:

- A small quantity of chemical toilet solution (some campsites insist on the 'green' bio solution only) should be added to the toilet cassette. This helps to break down waste and prevents the contents from smelling.

- Only use quick-disintegrating toilet paper (available from all camping and caravanning shops) suitable for toilet cassettes. It is designed to biodegrade much more quickly for easier emptying of the cassette.

- Only empty the contents where you see the sign for 'chemical WC'. A tap or hose for cleaning is usually provided. DO NOT use the hose at fresh water outlets or empty the contents down fresh water drains.

- Do not put sanitary towels or tampons into chemical toilets. You will be likely to block the cassette.

Blue or green?

There are two different kinds of chemical toilet fluids used for portable toilets, and appropriately they come in two different colours. The blue liquid (traditionally used) is based upon formaldehyde: a strong chemical that works well to help keep smells under control for days. However, it's not terribly friendly to the environment. Increasingly popular now is a green-coloured toilet fluid that works by using enzymes to break down the waste, but they do not last as long and require changing every couple of days. Though, frankly, who likes the idea of the waste lying around for much longer anyway?

Some campsites are now requesting that campers only use the more environmentally-friendly green coloured fluid when emptying portable toilets, and only at appropriate chemical WC waste disposal units.

> *You can also buy a pink-coloured fluid that is purely for keeping the toilet cassette deodorised. It will not actually break down the waste though.*

WILD CAMPING FACILITES

Wild camping with a tent naturally involves not having the convenience of a hot shower – or a flushing toilet – and rubbish collection on offer. To ensure that you have an enjoyable experience and leave the area just as you found it, try to follow these tips:

- Take all litter away with you and dispose of it in a suitable rubbish bin.

- Don't wash in a stream or lake with toiletries, but remove some water from the water source for washing. Do not empty your waste water back into the watercourse.

- To create a toilet area, dig a hole 10 to 15cm deep well away from water, footpaths, and your camping area. Ideally paper should be a fast-disintegrating toilet paper, as regular toilet paper takes a long time to decompose. Fill the hole back in afterwards.

✺ BASIC FIRST AID ✺

People relax when they go on holiday and that's when minor accidents can occasionally happen. The injuries you're most likely to come across while camping are:

- Cuts and grazes

- Nettle or wasp stings

- Trips and falls

- Burns and scalds

- Blisters (more from walking than camping)

- Food poisoning

Always take a first aid kit with you and include antihistamines, mosquito repellent, and sun cream, as well as basics such as painkillers and plasters. Make sure that you know what's in it, and top up any supplies that you've run out of as soon as you get home ready for next time. You can buy compact first aid kits put together especially for campers.

Tiny Camper Tip 🖊

If you have children camping with you, remember to take a small supply of age-appropriate painkillers.

CUTS AND GRAZES

Small cuts, grazes, and scratches in the countryside should be cleaned with an antiseptic wipe before tending to anything else, particularly if you are staying on a farm site where animals are present. If you haven't been vaccinated with a tetanus injection, then it's ideal to get one before you go camping.

For larger cuts and extensive bleeding, try to stop the blood flow by applying pressure to the area. This can be done by wrapping clothing or a towel quite tightly over the wound. If nothing is available to use as a dressing, apply pressure using clean fingers or a hand, depending on the size of the wound.

Get medical attention as soon as possible to clean and dress the wound properly.

TRIPS AND FALLS

The ground at campsites can invariably be uneven. Farmer's fields may have mole hills and rabbit holes that you simply don't see when running through the grass. Footpaths can be stony and just the additional time spent out in the fresh air gives rise to the opportunity for accidents.

If you 'twist an ankle' it may be painful to walk for a few minutes (therefore rest the ankle momentarily), but after that it should feel okay. If it continues to hurt, the ankle is likely to be sprained more seriously.

Pocket Fact 🏕

Sprains are tears to the elastic ligaments that hold joints or bones in place. They most often occur to ankles (when your foot accidently rolls over onto one side, perhaps by falling awkwardly on a rocky stone); knees (by falling awkwardly with the leg twisting from the knee as you fall); and the wrist (again, by falling and landing badly on your hands or wrist, and bending the wrist backwards).

A sprained joint may swell up and there could be bruising around the affected area.

To treat a sprain:

- Rest the limb. If you are out for a walk, try to use a stick or another person for support to avoid placing any pressure on the joint.

- Apply an ice pack to compress the joint. Chilled freezer blocks (especially the 'squishy' kind, rather than hard) are your most likely source at a campsite, but a bag of frozen peas will work well too. This will help to reduce any swelling and limit the bruising.

- Wrap the joint with a compression bandage.

- Elevate the affected limb and keep it rested without applying undue pressure, such as walking (ankles and knees) or using the affected hand (wrists).

BURNS AND SCALDS

Burns are heat injuries caused by flames or hot surfaces, while scalds are wet burns from hot liquids: one of the most common occurs from steam rising from a kettle or a pan of boiling water.

For first degree burns (where the epidermis is affected) and second degree burns (where both the epidermis and dermis are affected), treat with cool running water for as long as possible. If the skin blisters (with second degree burns), apply a dry, sterile dressing. For more serious burns, you should get medical treatment as soon as possible. Do not apply a grease or lotion. For sunburn see page 91.

Be extra vigilant about getting burnt when camping – cooking with gas stoves, boiling water/meals while cooking on uneven ground, campfires, and candles (children can so easily forget about a candle while reaching over a dinner table), can all be more dangerous outdoors so you need to be more cautious about preventing burns while camping.

Pocket Tip 🔥

Don't forget that any burned area will be extra sensitive to the sun and should be kept covered.

BLISTERS

These are more likely to come from excessive walking with poorly fitting boots, but they could arise from wearing shoes without socks or wearing flip-flops in the sunshine: both common occurrences on a campsite.

To prevent blisters on your feet while walking, make sure that you wear a comfortable pair of socks, and that your boots are made from a material that allow your feet to breathe such as Gore-tex. Your feet then have more chance of remaining cool. Check that the boots or shoes are the correct size for you – too tight or too loose and they will rub your feet, causing the skin to blister.

To treat a blister:

- Do not be tempted to pop the air sack to release the fluid as the blister might become infected.

- If and when the skin ruptures, allow the fluid to drain (but not by squeezing it out with grubby fingers).

- Apply an antiseptic cream to the blister with clean fingers and allow the skin to dry out by letting air reach the wound.

FOOD POISONING

Food poisoning, a form of *gastroenteritis*, is something that you really don't want at a campsite. It can cause severe vomiting and diarrhoea, neither of which you would wish to have when staying in a tent and using public loos. Painful abdominal cramps, headaches, and fever are also symptoms, and in severe cases it can be life threatening. The distress that food poisoning can cause is simply not worth the aggravation, especially as, in many instances, it can be avoided by following a few simple hygiene rules.

The easiest way to prevent food poisoning is by:

- Keeping your hands clean

- Making sure that you wash your hands (even if they look clean) before preparing and eating food

- Making sure that any food is kept at an appropriate temperature

- Checking that food is cooked through thoroughly

✸ DEALING WITH NATURE ✸ AND ANIMALS

Many campsites are based on farms that could have animals on site or in neighbouring fields. They are unlikely to be outwardly aggressive, but may be inquisitive and follow campers or hikers in the hope of food. Some animals, and birds such as swans and geese, will be particularly protective when looking after young, so do not approach if you can see that there is a parent animal or bird with babies.

Do not feed animals without permission from the farmer and be considerate. Farm animals do not like to be chased – encourage your children not to chase animals either on the farm or when out for a walk in the fields. Make sure that dogs are kept on a lead at all times while walking through fields of animals, and do not let them chase animals or birds either.

Bulls are rarely kept in a field by themselves, but you should always adhere to any 'No entry' signs at field entrances. They are there for your safety.

Always wash your hands after touching farm gates or when around farm animals. Encourage your children not to play with animal droppings and cowpats – they can carry infections.

Pocket Fact 🏕

It is very important to keep dogs on leads when going out for a walk around farms, particularly at a time of lambing, as a dog that is allowed to chase animals and poultry can cause them immense stress.

INSECTS

Most insects in the UK are simply irritating rather than deadly, but to avoid nasty bites and stings apply an insect repellent. Lemon-scented candles are useful in the evenings to keep mosquitoes away, but be careful when using candles in tents.

Pocket Tip 🔥

To avoid the dreaded Scottish 'midges' try spreading Avon's Skin So Soft body oil on your skin: it seems to keep them away!

Keep away from wasps' nests and beehives. If you do get stung, use an antihistamine cream such as Anthisan or antihistamine tablets. These creams are also useful for ant bites and nettle stings. Vinegar or lemon will counteract wasp or hornet stings too.

Bicarbonate of soda will help a bee sting. It's not the average ingredient that you take with you in your camping kitchen, so put a couple of teaspoons in a small pot and keep it in your first aid kit if you don't have an antihistamine cream.

If you can see the sting left behind by a bee, remove it with tweezers. Expect some localised swelling, pain, and redness.

> ## Emergencies
>
> *If breathing difficulties, swelling in the mouth or throat, chest pain, or faintness occurs having been stung, then urgent medical treatment is required as it could be an allergic reaction. Keep the airway open of the person affected, loosen any tight clothing, and call 999.*

Ticks

Ticks look like tiny beetles with eight legs, and are blood-sucking parasites that attach themselves to their host. They live in long grass, bushes, and some trees, and are less likely to live on short, well-mown grass. Brushing through long grass on a walk is when you are most likely to encounter them. You are unlikely to feel their bite, but they can transmit Lyme disease or tick-borne encephalitis: a debilitating illness that does not necessarily arise for some time after the bite but once contracted can last for months. Hosts can also contract meningitis.

There are a few places in the British Isles where they exist – the Scottish Highlands is one such place. Elsewhere in Europe, parts of Scandinavia, Eastern Europe, and the eastern parts of Germany are where they are most prevalent as well as parts of the USA and Canada.

You can be vaccinated against ticks but the cost is extremely expensive. If you are visiting an area where ticks are known to exist:

- Wear light coloured clothing (so that you can spot if a tick is there) that covers up your arms and legs in particular.

- Tuck trouser legs into socks.

- At the end of your walk or day, check for ticks – including under arms, at the backs of necks (the shirtline), the hairline, as well as legs and arms.

Treatment for ticks

If you do find a tick attached, do not grab at it as you may pull only a part away – leaving the head behind. Use a pair of tweezers to pull with a straight action, rather than at an angle, making sure that you also remove the head. The tick does need to be removed as soon as possible. You should seek medical advice if a tick is discovered attached to your skin; once removed, keep it to show the doctor.

SNAKES

There are just two snakes native to Britain. One of them, the grass snake, is not venomous. Its colour varies, but ranges from a deep khaki green to a muddy brown or almost black, and the skin may have blotchy markings.

The adder is the only indigenous poisonous snake in the UK. It has a black and yellow zigzag marking along the back.

Pocket Fact 🏕

A slow worm may look like a snake but it is actually a legless lizard.

Both the grass snake and adder are widespread throughout Britain and may be found on heathland or grass meadows. On hot summer days you may find them sunning themselves on stones or bare soil to receive radiated warmth. In winter they hibernate and may hide under logs, stones, or in compost heaps.

Watch out when walking in long grass, particularly in spring and autumn when they can be quite sluggish.

Treatment for snake bites

Adder bites are very rarely serious (a bite does not necessarily mean that it has been venomous), but you must seek medical treatment as soon as you can. Don't panic, try to immobilise the area that has been bitten, and get medical treatment from a hospital.

ANIMAL BITES AND STINGS

If you get bitten by any other animal, such as a dog, you should seek medical attention if the bite punctures the skin. Until you are able to get medical attention you should wash the wound with soap and water as soon as you can, dry it gently and cover it with a sterile dressing.

Rabies, a viral infection that affects animals such as dogs and foxes, does not exist in the UK (it's one of the reasons why you have to obtain a pet passport to take your pet in and out of the country). But it does exist on the continent and a rabid dog can pass the disease on. It's critical that you get attention urgently so that medical staff can treat a potential case effectively.

If you're by the sea, other stings to watch out for are jellyfish, sea urchins, and the 'Portuguese Man o' War', that can be mistaken for a jellyfish. Vinegar or salt water can help relieve the pain of box jellyfish, and vinegar and hot water will help sea urchin stings, but you must remove the spines as quickly as possible first. Do not use vinegar on Portuguese Man o' War stings as this can make the pain worse. You should get medical attention for all sea creature bites and stings.

POISONOUS PLANTS

Stinging nettles are the most common problem that you're likely to encounter while camping. The stings will appear as raised creamy white lumps with a red band around, and a stinging, tingling sensation will occur where the sting is.

Pocket Fact ⛺

Nettle stings can be soothed by rubbing a dock leaf on to the affected skin. They usually grow close together. For children the excitement of rushing around looking for a dock leaf will take their mind off the sting too.

Of course stinging nettles can be eaten (if you so wish!), but other plants are extremely poisonous when digested. These include:

- Deadly nightshade

- Rhubarb leaves

- Potato flowers

- Foxgloves

- Laburnum

- Privet

- Virginia Creeper

- Buttercup

- Yew (though you will see birds enjoying the red berries)

- Rhododendron

Tiny Camper Tip 🖊

Be aware of anything that children might pick up on a walk or in a garden, and teach them which plants are harmful. If these are eaten, seek medical advice urgently.

5

COOKING WHILE CAMPING

Campsite cooking, eating out of doors, and the socialising that surrounds mealtimes is as much a part of the camping experience as that unique feeling of going to bed and waking up under canvas. For some it's a liberating feeling to ditch the blender, the microwave, the sandwich toaster, and all the other paraphernalia that clutters the kitchen back at home, and return to a simpler way of cooking. Families that have barely rubbed shoulders in the kitchen, or passed a sideways glance around the dinner table for months, muck in and help prepare the campsite feast and even talk to one another between mouthfuls, enjoying one another's company while turning to a more holistic way of life, if only for a few days.

Cooking while camping gives you the chance to break away from your usual weekly shop and repetitive meal plans. Simple meals using fresh produce are often best when you only have limited facilities, and so you should organise your meals around whatever seasonal food you'll be able to find locally and plan to prepare it using fewer, or perhaps just different, resources. Cooking while camping doesn't have to mean eating baked beans from a tin, and with just a bit of careful planning and an open mind, you can prepare some tasty meals everyone can enjoy.

✱ WHAT FOOD TO BUY ✱

One of the best options is to take non-perishable items such as herbs, spices, and other ingredients (like tomato purée and balsamic vinegar) with you to accompany your meals, and buy perishable items such as eggs, sausages, and meat at your chosen location. That way you will have all the essentials for your meals, but be able to enjoy the freedom and fun of planning a meal around locally sourced ingredients.

Tips on buying food locally

- With the exception of the odd tin of baked beans and a tin of soup for 'emergencies', leave the tins and packets at home and try to shop locally. Tins are heavy to travel with, and you'll easily find a tin of this or that wherever you're travelling to if you really need it.

- By buying local produce you'll be helping the local economy and food producers, and having fun choosing what you'll eat that day depending on the weather and the mood. You never know, it might change your daily eating habits and the way you do your food shopping for life.

- Work out a menu before you go that cuts down on the need to store lots of perishable food as it will save storage space in your tent and car. But don't be a slave to your menu plan: if you see something that interests you, buy it and have fun cooking something new.

- Depending on where you are staying, look out for regional specialities to try something different. At the seaside, try fresh mackerel and sardines – these are divine cooked simply on the edge of a campfire. Inland, look for 'proper' sausages in a nearby farm shop, or a chunk of locally made cheese to have with some freshly made bread.

- If the campsite has a website, see if they offer food hampers upon arrival. Some do and they can offer a wonderful selection of local produce and camping essentials such as bread, milk, eggs, and locally-reared meats including bacon and sausages.

Pocket Tip 🔥

Why not go back to your hunter-gatherer roots and, at the start of the day, assign a taskforce of meal providers (children will love to get involved with this) to locate the ingredients required for an evening meal? It could be a trip to the local farmer's market, a trip to the beach with a fishing net, or picking blackberries from the hedgerows down the lane.

✸ WHAT FOOD CAN BE FOUND ✸ AT A CAMPSITE

This all depends on the kind of campsite that you're going to. A large campsite catering for many campers will undoubtedly have a large shop selling as much as you'd find in a small supermarket, including fresh bread and rolls.

Pocket Tip 🔥

Some campsites that sell fresh bread in the morning may ask you to order it the night before. Check upon arrival so that you don't end up without breakfast. If you're booking a campsite before you leave, check where you can buy food and what is available, whether on site or nearby.

Some campsites may have a bakery van that delivers fresh bread around the campsite in the mornings, and a fish and chip van that calls in the evening (usually only once a week though). On European sites you can often find a pizza van or a *rôtisserie* van selling cooked chicken.

Small farm campsites may not sell anything at all, although you can usually buy a few eggs and maybe a jar of homemade jam.

Pocket Fact 🏕

There are over 500 farmer's markets held regularly throughout the UK, selling food and other items that are produced within a few miles of where they're being sold. You can buy anything from fresh meat, fish, eggs, dairy produce, bread and cakes, jams and honey, fruit and vegetables, sold direct from the producer. So you're bound to find something that you like, while saving on the miles the food has travelled too.

✳ WHAT FOODS TO PACK ✳

If you camp regularly, keep a box of staple foods that is ready to go, so that you don't need to keep raiding the kitchen cupboards for those last-minute camping trips.

Suggestions for your box include:

- Tea and coffee
- Hot chocolate
- Sugar
- Ketchup
- Tinned beans
- Stock cubes
- Pasta and rice
- Salt and pepper pots

Top the supplies up when you return home so that it's all ready to go again.

When you're about to set off on your trip take a few essential perishable foods, such as milk and eggs, to get you started, but remember the points about shopping locally for perishable ingredients.

Pocket Tip 🔥

Before you leave home, prepare something that can be eaten instantly when you arrive at the campsite, or that is ready for the first evening meal, as you'll be busy unpacking and erecting a tent and may not be in the mood to think about cooking that first night. Put the meal in the cooler together with an ice pack and a bottle of wine, and you'll have supper all ready for when you arrive.

Obviously if you're going wild camping or know there won't be many facilities at your campsite, it's best to take a few simple ingredients that you can put together in different ways to create a variety of meals. Tinned or dehydrated ingredients with lots of herbs and spices are probably your best bet so you can be sure that nothing goes off.

✳ HOW TO TRANSPORT AND ✳ STORE FOOD

Arriving at your chosen campsite with a packet of crushed biscuits and a bottle of milk that has leaked all over the back seat of the car is not ideal. Here are some top tips to ensure it doesn't happen:

● Packing your food tightly in boxes rather than higgledy-piggledy in plastic carrier bags will help.

● Use plastic containers for transporting as they pack (and stack) well and are lightweight. Store all foods in containers while on site too, preferably airtight, to prevent creepy crawlies from reaching them. Keep raw and cooked foods separate and any strong smelling foods such as garlic away from other produce. Garlic and butter do not mix, unless you're making garlic bread!

● Avoid leaving food lying around – it may be essential in Canada for your own safety against bears, but even much closer to home, the smell of food can attract insects and the neighbour's dog when you're not looking.

- Use an insulated coolbox or camping fridge for storing dairy produce and meat. If you have the space, take a coolbox (the sides should be at least 3cm thick) with you when you're out during the day with the car in case you come across some tasty goodies for the evening meal. It will keep meat and fish fresh until you get back to camp.

- If you have food stored with freezer blocks, keep storage lids closed and do not re-freeze food if you suspect it has been thawing.

Pocket Tip 🔥

You can buy coolboxes that will work from 12 volts; simply plug it into your 12-volt lighter and the contents will remain cool while you're driving. Don't forget, though, that if you run the box from your car battery when parked, you may return to a flat battery.

Backpackers' food

Backpackers will need to think carefully about weight, and consider carrying lightweight, instant meals with them that just require boiling water to turn them from a dehydrated powder to a nourishing meal. The sachets of dried ingredients don't always look that appealing, but on a wet and windy night they can taste like amber nectar!

Don't forget to take something sweet such as Kendal Mint Cake for instant energy in case you need it.

✳ HOW TO PREPARE FOOD ✳

Preparing food and cooking outdoors can be a different experience to the comfort of your own kitchen, where you know exactly where to find every utensil and where there are plenty of work surfaces. On a campsite though – or while wild camping – you're not necessarily going to know what facilities are on offer to you. Find out what cooking facilities are available before you leave home and plan your meals accordingly: you don't want to bring all of the ingredients for a barbecue to find out they're banned.

Food safety and hygiene tips

- When using either a barbecue or a camping stove, make sure that it is on level ground – and that the ground remains level. Every time you use any cooking equipment, check that the leg of the table upon which the stove is sitting has not sunk into the ground. You do not need a pan of boiling water falling off the stove on to you or anyone else.

- Be much more vigilant about children playing around you when cooking and preparing food. They may be aware about not charging about in the kitchen at home, but the freedom of an outdoor space can stop brains from thinking about 'kitchen' safety. Better still, have little ones help out with the cooking, and then they won't be running around when the spuds are boiling!

- You are less likely to have space in which to prepare food, so take extra care to avoid cross-contamination during preparation. Use a child's thin, plastic tablemat as a chopping board. They're lightweight to transport and it means you can take two or three to use as separate boards for chopping meat, vegetables, and bread.

- Do your best to keep flies and creepy crawlies off food by keeping it all in sealed containers, covering with a clean tea towel as you serve up, or storing in a coolbox.

- If you're using an insulated coolbox that is not plugged into an electric hook-up, have a spare set of freezer blocks. Two sets means that you can always keep one set freezing while the other set is in use, preventing your chilled food from warming up while your blocks are being chilled. This is vitally important if you are camping somewhere with very hot weather, as food that is not being kept at a constant temperature is more likely to develop problematic bacteria.

- It sounds very basic but don't forget to wash your hands before preparing food, even with some cold running water if you don't have soap. It can be easy to forget when you're living outside, having been on a walk through the woods picking up sticks for the dog and conkers for the children. Toughening up the immune system is great, but no one wants food poisoning, especially living in a tent.

- Keeping meat and dairy food chilled is the most important consideration to staying safe. A warm bottle of lemonade or beer may not be as thirst-quenching as a cold one, but it won't kill you; contaminated meat that has not been stored correctly could. Likewise, make sure that food has been heated thoroughly, by allowing sauces and soups to simmer (though do not boil as it will impair the flavour). To check that meat (especially chicken) is thoroughly cooked, pierce it with a fork or skewer; the juices should run clear.

- Any food waste should be disposed of frequently to avoid attracting flies, wasps, and other irritants. Don't leave it overnight – clear up after a meal and dispose of the waste in an appropriate rubbish bin before you go to bed. Throwing it into the nearby hedge or around the campsite will only attract other undesirables, such as rodents. In certain countries where predators are life-threatening, if you cannot dispose of food waste instantly, keep it (and any other food – separate from the waste) in a car, or hung from a tree well away from where you are sleeping.

Cooking in a tent

For safety, cook outside of the tent or under a gazebo whenever you can. If it's pouring with rain and there is a camper's kitchen on the campsite, use that if you can, rather than the tent.

If you have to cook in the tent, keep the stove away from the tent walls and make sure that you have plenty of ventilation to prevent a build-up of gas. Ideally cook under an awning or porch. If your tent only has one door, do not cook there as it could block your main fire escape.

Never leave a stove unattended when cooking inside a tent. In fact, never leave a stove unattended at all on a campsite, where the potential is for someone else's child or dog to wander onto your pitch and be injured.

Don't cook in a tent while someone is sleeping as the chances of waking them quickly in the event of an emergency could cause major problems.

Pocket Tip 🔥

Have a fire extinguisher to hand, and know how to use it.

What equipment to use

- If you do not have a camping fridge or coolbox, use a bucket of cold water as a simple cooler. Soaking a towel and draping it over the top will make it even more effective.

- You won't want to cart around an entire picnic set when wild camping, so eating straight out of the cooking pot will become the norm. Look for camping pans with folding handles to save space in a rucksack. If the cutlery is non-existent and eating with your fingers is not an option, find two thin green (living) sticks, clean off the bark with a sharp knife, and use them as chopsticks. These can also be used as kebab skewers and toasting forks with an open campfire.

- Melamine 'crockery' and plastic glasses prevent breakages. No one wants to find a piece of glass embedded in the ground by treading or falling on it.

Pocket Tip 🔥

If you can't stand drinking out of a cheap plastic glass, you can buy better quality glasses that look and have (almost) the same feel as glass when you're drinking. They cost a little bit more but they can be worth it, particularly if you've opted for a special bottle of wine.

BARBECUES

Barbecues can turn campsite cooking from a basic beans-in-a-pan experience to a gourmet dinner. But without the comforts of nipping back into the kitchen at home for this or that, using a barbecue at a campsite can be a slightly different affair.

- Do not use barbecues directly on the grass at a campsite – especially the instant kind in its own aluminium tray (most campsites tend to have a rule about the use of barbecues, so check before you light one). If your barbecue doesn't have legs, lift it off the ground using wood, bricks, or a purpose-built stand. The heat from the base of the barbecue will kill the grass and campsite owners will not thank you for it.

- Charcoal briquettes tend to last longer and deliver a more even heat than traditional charcoal. Briquettes are ready for cooking once they have turned grey, while traditional charcoal is ready as soon as any flames have died down; though leave it too long and the charcoal will not have enough residual heat to cook meat thoroughly. With kettle barbecues (those with a lid), once the charcoal or briquettes are up to temperature, arrange the fuel around the outside of the kettle before the grate and lid goes on.

- Using a gas barbecue is perhaps more convenient (remember to check your gas levels before leaving home) and is quicker to get cooking with, but it's not quite the same as that smoky barbecue taste that you get with a traditional charcoal barbecue.

- Do not use too much lighting liquid with a barbecue or the taste will taint your food. Look for instant lighting fuels that just require a match.

- It's the fat from the meat and vegetable juices that help to keep barbecued food tender. Brush any foods that don't contain their own fat with some melted butter or oil.

✦ WATER ✦

All campsites, however small, are expected to provide a fresh water supply, so there should be no need to take any with you other than a reasonable amount for your journey. In certain countries it is advisable to purify the water before drinking and for certain activities such as cleaning teeth.

- Campsites will keep separate taps and drains for drinking water and for waste water.

- Never fill up your water bottles from a tap or hose that is being used for waste water and disposal.

- When you can, use wide-mouthed containers to fill up with drinking water so that the tap does not need to touch the container. Never stick a hose into your drinking water container – you don't know where it has been!

Pocket Tip 🔥
Keep and re-use large capacity wide mouth water or squash bottles. They are convenient and safe to fill through the wide mouth, usually have a sturdy carrying handle, and are fully recyclable.

When wild camping, look for a fresh water source such as a mineral spring or the outflow of a lake. Do not drink untreated water collected downstream of a town or village, or where the water looks stagnant. Collapsible water holders are great for backpacking.

PURIFYING WATER

If you're concerned about the quality of the water to drink, purifying it is safer than using sterilisation tablets. On a campsite, you can use a water filter in the same way as you would at home. If wild camping, take some water purification tablets with you. These can be bought at many camping shops.

As a last resort, boil the water for 10 minutes to kill off bacteria.

Pocket Fact 🏕

If you are planning to visit a country where you're unsure of the water quality, you can check if it's advisable to find alternative drinking water on the Foreign & Commonwealth Office website: www.fco.gov.uk.

✾ RECIPES ✾

Here are some tasty recipes to try out while camping:

BREAKFAST

All-in-one cooked breakfast

Ingredients
Pork sausages
Bacon
Mushrooms, chopped
Fresh tomatoes, chopped into quarters
Baked beans
1 tsp olive oil

Equipment
One hob or stove plate
Saucepan (size dependent upon number of people cooking for)
Sharp knife
Wooden spoon

Method

1. Place 1 tsp of olive oil into a saucepan and heat gently. Chop the sausages into approximately 2.5cm pieces and cook for 12 minutes, moving them around the pan regularly to prevent from burning and until they have an even brown skin. Drain any excess fat (good quality sausages should not produce any fat of their own; the teaspoon of olive oil is merely to prevent the sausage pieces from sticking to the base of the pan). Remove the sausages from the pan and put to one side.

2. Roughly chop the bacon rashers into small pieces and cook for 5 minutes. Remove from the pan and put to one side with the sausages.

3. Using any residual fat from the bacon, place the chopped mushrooms in the pan and brown them over a high heat, tossing regularly to prevent sticking.

4. Add the fresh tomatoes and cook for a further 2 to 3 minutes.

5. Reduce the stove to a moderate heat and add the baked beans to the saucepan, heating gently.

6. Return the sausages and bacon bits to the pan and stir gently (you don't want a mash) into the mushroom, tomato and baked bean mix. Cook for a further 5 minutes on a moderate heat, stirring occasionally. Do not let the mixture boil or the flavours will be impaired.

This recipe can also be used as a hearty and warming filling for a baked potato at suppertime – great in cooler autumn temperatures.

American pancakes

Ingredients

(makes approximately 8 to 12 pancakes)
100g plain flour
1 dessert spoon baking powder (as this is an ingredient you're unlikely to find in a campsite shop or that you consider as an essential item to take with you from home, it's not strictly necessary within the recipe, but it does make the pancakes lighter and fluffier)

2 large eggs, beaten
150 ml milk
15g butter, melted
1 tsp sugar
Pinch of salt
Butter or lard for frying
Maple syrup, fresh fruit (blueberries and strawberries are great) or topping of your choice

Equipment

Hob or stove plate
Frying pan
Metal/wooden spatula or fish slice (not plastic as it will melt)
Mixing bowl
Wooden spoon
Measuring jug

Method

1. Put the flour, baking powder, sugar and salt into a large bowl (sieved if you happen to have one – it will make the pancakes lighter), and make a well in the middle to receive the egg.

2. Gradually stir in the egg, milk and melted butter a little at a time. Beat vigorously (particularly if you haven't been able to sieve the flour).

3. Heat a knob of butter in the frying pan and drop separate tablespoons of batter mixture into the pan, cooking 2 to 3 pancakes at a time.

4. When the top side of each pancake is bubbling, turn it over and cook the other side until golden brown.

5. Serve drizzled with maple syrup or your choice of topping.

Tiny Camper Tip 🖊

Children of all ages love these pancakes for breakfast. It's a great recipe to get them involved in the preparation too.

LUNCH

Tricolore salad

Ingredients

(serves 2)

A mixture of salad leaves
2 fresh tomatoes
1 large ball of mozzarella cheese
1 medium avocado
Fresh basil
50g pancetta, chopped into pieces (streaky bacon will do if you cannot get the very thin pancetta)
1 slice of bread
1tsp olive oil

Salad dressing

Mix 1 tbsp olive oil with 1tbsp balsamic vinegar or lemon juice, salt and pepper and a teaspoon of a fruit chutney for some zing.

Equipment

Hob or stove plate
Chopping board
Scissors
Large serving bowl or plate

Method

1. Preheat a frying pan with a teaspoon of olive oil. Cut the slice of bread into small cubes and toss in the olive oil, cooking on a high heat until the croutons are golden brown. Toss frequently and watch constantly or they will burn very quickly! Put to one side.

2. Place a selection of salad leaves over the base of the serving bowl or plate.

3. Chop the fresh tomatoes into small pieces, removing the core, and place around the edge of the serving plate.

4. Rip the mozzarella cheese into small pieces and place on top of the salad leaves in the centre of the serving plate.

5. Prepare the avocado by cutting into quarters, removing the stone, then peeling away the skin from the flesh. Cut each quarter into thin slices or small pieces. Add to the centre of the salad plate.

6. Using the same pan as for the croutons (wiping away any breadcrumbs with a piece of kitchen towel), cook the chopped pancetta over a high heat for 2 to 3 minutes until crispy. Pancetta will cook in its own fat so there is no need to add extra oil or fat for cooking. Add the pancetta pieces to the centre of the salad.

7. Sprinkle the croutons onto the salad. Rip some fresh basil leaves into pieces over the salad and drizzle with a dressing. Serve immediately.

Eton Mess

This is a good dessert for a first day at a campsite, if you bring the meringues with you from home, or it's great if you're lucky enough to find some homemade meringues to buy near your campsite. It's quick and simple to make and is even more fabulous if you can find some locally grown fruit and maybe buy some cream direct from a farm – it tastes infinitely better than anything you can buy in a supermarket.

Ingredients
Meringues (1 to 2 per person, depending on the size of the meringue)
1 large pot fresh double or whipping cream
Fresh strawberries (or raspberries or a mixture of soft berry fruits)

Equipment
Large mixing bowl
Sharp knife
Balloon whisk

Method
1. Whisk the cream in the mixing bowl until it forms soft peaks.

2. Break up the meringues into the whipped cream.

3. Hull the strawberries and slice. Add these, or any other berries you happen to have been able to buy, to the cream and meringues. Mix together very gently. Serve immediately (or the meringues will disintegrate into the cream).

Pocket Fact 🏕

Strawberries are traditionally in season throughout June and early July. Try to find a pick-your-own farm where you may be able to select the variety. Throughout France, but particularly in the Dordogne region, you can buy an early variety throughout May known as 'Gariguette'. Long and pointy in shape, they have one of the sweetest tastes of all strawberries. Spain is one of the largest growers of strawberries in Europe while in Austria, Switzerland, and Scandinavia, look out for the tiny 'alpine' strawberries with a unique flavour.

DINNER

Entree: Chicken breast fillets with mushrooms and bacon

Ingredients

(serves 4)

4 skinless chicken breasts

150g mushrooms, very finely chopped (chestnut mushrooms give a really good nutty, woody flavour to this dish)

4 rashers of thin pancetta (ideally) or streaky bacon

Knob of butter

Equipment

Hob or stove plate

Barbecue (with tongs)

Saucepan

Chopping board

Sharp knife

Baking foil

Method

1. Preheat a small saucepan and melt a knob of butter. Chop the mushrooms into tiny pieces and add to the pan, then stir and cover to allow the mushrooms to sweat. Remove the liquid that remains and leave to one side to make gravy.

2. Score the underside of each chicken breast with a sharp knife and stuff with a quantity of the cooked mushrooms. Fold the sides of the chicken breast (made by scoring it) back over to encase the mushroom filling.

3. Wrap each chicken breast with a rasher of pancetta or streaky bacon and then place each one onto lightly buttered, individual pieces of baking foil. Wrap the parcels up and place on the barbecue, cooking for approximately 25 to 30 minutes.

4. If you happen to have a bottle of red wine open, you can make tasty gravy by cooking 2 very finely chopped shallots (or 1 onion) in a teaspoon of olive oil in a saucepan. If you have any pancetta or any mushroom mixture left over this can also be added. Once the shallots have softened, add a dessert spoon of plain flour and stir (it will look quite 'stodgy' at this stage). Gradually add the liquid that was left over from cooking the mushrooms and stir continuously until the mixture is smooth. Add a glug of red wine and seasoning, stir until it thickens and leave to cook gently for 10 minutes.

Pocket Tip ☘

To check that each chicken breast is cooked thoroughly, unwrap the foil parcel and prod the meat with a fork or sharp knife. If the juices that run out are pink, it needs more cooking time; if they run as a clear liquid, it is ready to serve.

Dessert: Honeyed baked bananas in foil

Ingredients

(serves 4)

4 bananas

4 tbsp sugar (ideally Demerara) or honey

Lemon juice
Whipped cream, crème fraiche or mascarpone cheese to serve

Equipment
Barbecue (and tongs)
Baking foil
Knife

Method
1. Lightly butter 4 pieces of foil, each large enough to wrap around 1 banana.

2. Peel the banana and place it onto the foil. Sprinkle with a tablespoon of sugar or drizzle with a tablespoon of honey, squeeze over some lemon juice, and wrap up the foil into a parcel.

3. Place on the barbecue and bake for 30 minutes. The banana should be soft and gooey when ready to eat. Unwrap, taking care not to lose the delicious toffee-like sauce that will have developed, and serve immediately (though the bananas will be very hot) with some whipped cream, crème fraiche, or mascarpone cheese for some extra bite.

Pocket Tip 🔥

Demerara sugar is great for this as it caramelises as it melts, creating a delicious toffee sauce around the banana. Otherwise honey works just as well.

SNACKS

Griddled sweetcorn

Ingredients
Corn on the cob (one per person)
Butter

Equipment
Barbecue and tongs

Method

1. This is as simple as placing each sweetcorn cob onto a barbecue with medium to hot coals, and leaving to cook for 10 minutes.

2. Brush with butter part way through cooking to help keep the corn moist (brush too early and the sweetcorn kernels will simply burn before they're cooked right through).

Potato wedges

Ingredients

Waxy potatoes (1 per person)
Seasoning such as mixed herbs, paprika or a ready-prepared mix
Olive oil

Equipment

Barbecue
Baking sheet (preferably with holes)
Baking foil
Sharp knife

Method

1. Leaving the skins on, chop each potato into bite-sized wedges.

2. Drizzle with olive oil and make sure that each piece is well coated.

3. Dip each potato wedge into a bowl of your chosen seasoning.

4. Place on a baking sheet, layered with foil, and cover, either with a barbecue lid (if using a kettle barbecue) or with another layer of foil. Cook for 45 minutes to an hour.

5. Serve with your favourite dip.

TREATS

Marshmallows are the obvious classic for camping, toasted on a campfire. You'll need a long-handled toasting fork or long kebab skewers and it only takes a few seconds to toast a marshmallow. Wait until the fire has burnt down to its embers before toasting marshmallows – roaring flames will ruin your marshmallow as well as your skin, eyebrows, or anything else that it comes into contact with and can be very dangerous.

Keep small children well back from the fire, and if you receive the attention of children from other families (and you almost certainly will if you're dishing out marshmallows!) get permission from their parents for them to be around the fire as well. While you don't want to be a party pooper, there's nothing to spoil a party as feeling responsible for someone else's child who's just burnt their mouth – or hand – on a toasted marshmallow.

Pocket Tip 🔥

Remember that the fire will be very, very hot even once it has died down, and you should toast your marshmallow at arm's length on a long skewer. Remember too that the toasted marshmallow gets very hot and should be left to cool before eating. NEVER put the marshmallow straight into your mouth while on the skewer.

Of course not all campsites allow campfires and it may be considered too risky with very small children, so here are some edible games that you can play with untoasted marshmallows.

Marshmallows on a string

Using a needle and thread or cotton string (not hairy string), thread five to 10 marshmallows onto individual strings – one for each player. Hang the strings from the branch of a tree so that each player can reach the marshmallows without using their hands. The winner is the first player to eat all their marshmallows.

Marshmallow kebabs

Have the children create their own kebab masterpiece using marshmallows and fruits – such as strawberries, grapes, chunks of kiwi fruit and pineapple. Chocolate brownies are good for this too.

Marshmallow draughts

Draw a chequered pattern onto a piece of paper or card. Separate equal quantities of pink and white marshmallows and use them to play draughts on the patterned board. Players who capture a draught (marshmallow) are entitled to eat it.

And for the ultimate indulgence:

Chocolate fondue

Ingredients

200g bar of plain chocolate
1/4 pint double cream
3 tbsp honey or golden syrup
Marshmallows
Fresh fruit such as strawberries, orange segments, banana chunks, kiwi or peach slices
Any other treats such as chocolate brownies, peppermint creams, and biscuits

Equipment

Hob or stove plate
Saucepan
Metal or glass bowl (that will fit on the top of the pan)
Chopping board and sharp knife (if preparing fruit)
Kebab skewers or forks for serving

Method

1. Place a saucepan with a small quantity of water on to a low heat on the stove. Cover with the metal or glass bowl.

2. Break the chocolate into chunks and place into the bowl. Heat very gently and slowly.

3. Once the chocolate has melted, add the double cream and honey or golden syrup and stir. Lift from the heat immediately, remembering that a rush of hot steam will rise from the pan as you do so.

4. Serve with a selection of treats to dip.

Pocket Tip 🔥

If young children are not involved (who says adults can't have fun?) why not add a splash of rum or brandy into the fondue once all the other ingredients have been mixed together? It makes the fondue a decadently warming treat for those autumnal camping expeditions when the evenings turn cooler.

6

CAMPING ACTIVITIES

There are certain activities that seem to be synonymous with camping, such as sitting around a campfire, a game of badminton, or a good walk. Here we've provided ideas and tips for games to play, items to bring with you (and what to leave at home), activities with nature, and making the most of campfires with a traditional sing-song or ghost story.

✸ NO-EQUIPMENT ACTIVITES ✸

Some of the most enjoyable activities when camping are the simplest, and don't require any equipment at all. They may be the sorts of things you are unable to do – or don't do – at home.

Top five camping activities (that don't require equipment)

1. *Folding back the door of the tent and looking at the night sky*
2. *Watching a brilliant red sunset and a large moon rising*
3. *Chatting to friends and family without the distractions of home life*
4. *Enjoying a stunning view*
5. *Listening to the gentle rain on the tent while feeling cosy inside*

✸ GAMES TO PLAY WITH ✸ LIMITED RESOURCES

You can't rely all the time on a cloudless night or a stunning sunset, or even a campsite with a view. Sometimes you need to make up some entertainment.

French cricket

Equipment required

A cricket bat, tennis or badminton racket – or even a stick from the woods
A lightweight ball of any size (the smaller the size, the harder the game), or an object such as a pine cone

Number of players

2–5 players of any age, providing they can walk

Rules

One person is the batsman: they must stand, feet together, on one spot. Another person is the bowler. The bowler aims the ball at the batsman's legs. If it hits the legs below the knee, the batsman is out.

The batsman must try to defend their legs by hitting the ball. They are not allowed to move their feet at any point, although they can twist their body to protect the back of their legs. If they hit the ball, they have scored a 'run'. If any other players (fielders) catch the ball, the batsman is out. The ball must be bowled from the direction in which the ball is hit.

Players take it in turns to be batsman, bowler, and fielders. The winner is the person with the most runs.

Giant tiddlywinks

Equipment required

A bucket or can
A ball, disk, lightweight sticks, conkers or feathers

Number of players

Any number, any age

Rules

Place a bucket, box or can into position and mark a line some distance away. Players must accurately throw the item into the vessel. The game can be made harder or easier according to the age group by: furthering or reducing the distance between the throwing line and the vessel; using a smaller or larger vessel (a tin can for teenagers and adults for example, and a large trug bucket for young children); or reducing the size and weight of the object to be thrown (acorns and feathers for grown-ups, and a large ball for children).

The winner is the player with the most number of strikes into the vessel.

Aunt Sally

Equipment required
A tall pin with a flat surface on top (this could be something like an upturned log in the woods)
A 'dolly' such as a stone, empty tin can or plastic bottle
Five sticks

Number of players
Any number, any age providing they can stand and throw

Rules
The dolly is placed on the pin or log. If using a wall, check that nothing behind it can be damaged and that you can retrieve the sticks and the dolly.

Players take it in turns to stand behind a designated line in front of the dolly and throw the sticks, one at a time, at it. The aim is to get a clean strike using as few sticks as possible, knocking the dolly from the pin. Score points with the sticks: five for the first stick, four for the second and so on.

The winner is the player with the most points after a given time or number of goes.

Note: this game should be played away from pitches. You do not want to be held responsible for hitting someone's car or caravan.

Who am I?

Equipment required
None

Number of players

Any number, any age, so long as they can talk!

Rules

One player (the detective) leaves the area, while the others (the court) decide which well-known person they represent (you can alter this to any character for younger players). The detective returns and asks each court member in turn one question only, which must be answered with a 'yes' or 'no'. After a set number of questions, the detective has three guesses to name the person – scoring a point for a correct guess. The winner is the player with the most points after a designated number of rounds.

✸ OTHER FUN THINGS TO BRING ✸

If you're staying at a campsite for longer than a couple of nights, you may feel the need to rely on more than what nature can provide.

Top five classic things to take to a campsite

1. *A football*
2. *Swingball*
3. *Tennis rackets or badminton rackets (lighter to carry)*
4. *A pack of playing cards*
5. *Board games*

BOARD GAMES

Before loading up the car with excess 'stuff', consider how long you are going away for: are you really going to have time to use *all* that equipment or will half of it suffice?

Pocket Tip 🔥

Take board games with you that don't include lots of little pieces that could get lost in the grass easily. You'll get frustrated with losing them and they're not that nice to stand on with bare feet. And there's nothing like being woken up by a plastic aircraft carrier in your sleeping bag after a late night game of Battleships.

Suggested games with larger pieces (or take magnetic versions where the pieces stay on the board):

● Connect Four

● Chess

● Draughts (magnetic)

● Scrabble (magnetic)

● Shut the Box

● Pictionary

● Twister

● Jenga

● Dominoes

● Trivial Pursuit (travel version without game pieces)

BOOKS

Many campsites offer a book swap facility, where you can take a book away in replacement for giving one back. They're usually well-thumbed paperbacks of popular reads, and campsites are generally happy to receive additional cast-offs to bulk out the selection.

There's no need to take an entire library of books with you unless you're an avid reader. You may not wish to carry field guides on every tree, wild flower, bird, and butterfly but a general 'spotters' guide is useful if you're interested in finding out more about the wildlife in the area (see page 138). A travel guide to the area in which you're staying is also a useful read to have. And, of course, don't forget your *Camping Pocket Bible!*

Pocket Tip 🔥

You may not get to see a starry sky that often depending on where you live, so take advantage while you're in the great out-doors. A guide to the night sky will show you what to look for and where to look for it depending on the seasons.

WHEN BOREDOM SETS IN

You need never be bored when camping. There is always going to be something to do, whether it's planning and cooking an al fresco feast, lying back with a good book, or investigating the local footpaths. Even the washing up needs doing at some point!

But for those moments when you or family members might be waiting for something to happen, it helps to have something prepared.

- Take some glow sticks with you. When it's dark children love them for games, and adults can wrap them around a glass to identify their drink. You can also use them for identification purposes in night-time team games (each team wears a different colour), or after-dark treasure hunts.

- Have a pack of playing cards handy. Any number of people can join in a game of cards and Solitaire can be played by just one person.

- Have a special 'job' that is saved only if boredom sets in. It might be something extremely mundane such as sorting colour-coordinated clothes pegs or cleaning boots, in which case you'll find anything to avoid doing it and therefore not get bored. Or it might be a really exciting 'job', which will prevent you from getting bored at all.

Tiny Camper Tip

If your child complains of boredom are they actually over-tired? A quick lie down or a little daytime nap might be all that's required to perk them up again.

⊛ OUT AND ABOUT IN NATURE ⊛

How are you on the differences between a beech tree and a birch? Can you tell the footprint of a badger from that of a fox? And do you know the difference between a blue tit and a coal tit?

Knowing what's around you can really add pleasure to a walk. But if you don't want to take umpteen field guides with you, then take a photo and look it up when you get back home. You might also need to make a few notes. Here are some tips on features to take note of.

Recognising birds

- The size – compare it to something you're familiar with (especially as a close-up photo might not provide anything to compare its size with)

- General colours – important if you don't have your camera with you

- Any obvious markings

- Size, shape and colour of bill, legs, tail or neck

Pocket Fact 🏕

It is illegal to take the eggs from the nest of most wild birds. They are protected by the Protection of Birds Act 1954.

Animal tracks

- Location of footprint – in a wood, close to a river, on the beach etc

- Size of footprint – width and depth

- Shape of footprint – hoof, paw, bird's foot (webbed or individual toes?)

- How many – toes, claw marks, hoof imprints?

- Distance apart of each print

- In pairs or staggered prints?

Identifying trees

- Its size and shape

- Leaves or needles – shape and colour

- Bark – texture (take a rubbing using paper and pencil or crayon) and colour

- Flowers, fruit and seeds – blossom, pine cones or berries

Identifying flowers

- Size – height of plant plus size of individual flowers

- Colour – of flowers and leaves (dark green, silver etc)

- Shape of flower and petals – bell, cup, clusters, number of petals

- Habitat – coastal, riverbank, roadside, hedgerow etc

- Time of year it's flowering

Pocket Tip 🔥
Never pick wild flowers. Some are protected species.

⊛ BY THE FIRESIDE ⊛

SONGS

The campfire's burning, the marshmallows are toasting and everyone has gathered around for a sing-song. It may sound a touch old-fashioned in this modern world, but you'd be amazed how many people will join in the singing after an initial bout of apprehension.

Many campfire songs have materialised from the Scout Movement. Brownies, Guides, Cubs, and Scouts have all been brought up singing traditional fireside songs. They never leave you. Here are some of the most popular:

- *She'll Be Comin' Round the Mountain*

- *The Ants Go Marching*

- *Ging Gang Gooly*

- *Kumbayah (Come By Here)*

- *There's a Hole in My Bucket*

- *Home on the Range*

- *If You're Happy and You Know It*

- *BINGO*

- *Alice the Camel*

- *Old Macdonald Had a Farm*

Of course, the most appropriate song to start off a campfire sing-song is *Campfire's Burning*. To the tune of *London's Burning*, it can be sung in a round if there is a sufficient number of people.

Campfire's Burning

Campfire's Burning, Campfire's Burning

Draw in Nearer, Draw in Nearer

In the gloamin', In the gloamin'

Come sing and be merry

To add to the general din, you can supply makeshift instruments too:

- Wooden spoons clicked together

- A chocolate selection tin for a drum

- Metal tent pegs tapped together

- Blocks of wood tapped together

Please note: not every camper wishes to hear your musical entertainment!

Campers generally accept some singing may go on at a campsite and they may well accept an accompanying guitar, but they will be unhappy if the singing and 'music' goes on well into the night and may even make a complaint if it disturbs the peace after a certain time.

Other campers possibly won't enjoy your makeshift instruments – these may be best left to those who have a campsite to themselves.

Be considerate and respectful to your fellow campers, the campsite owners and their neighbours, whom they have to continue to live with side-by-side long after you've packed up and gone home!

GHOST STORIES

Spinning a good yarn is a traditional part of sitting around a campfire, and the ambience of a crackling fire creates the right mood for a ghost story. Some like to be deliciously scared before they climb into their tent at night, while others will hate the idea. Before you begin narrating a story, think about the age of your audience and ask yourself if it is suitable for all. Remember that ghost stories are not crime thrillers; your audience wants to be scared but not disturbed.

A ghost story collection

A Ghost Story by Mark Twain. Written in 1903, it tells the story of a stranger who comes to town and lodges in a dilapidated old building in New York. As he prepares for sleep, eerie sights and sounds build.

The Signalman by Charles Dickens. The most famous of Dickens' ghost stories, and a regular contender for the most chilling ghost story ever, it's the tale of a spectre warning a signalman of impending disaster. Written in 1865, Dickens had been involved in a serious train crash the previous year.

A Christmas Carol by Charles Dickens. If you've pulled out the extra blankets and gone for a winter camping break, this one's for you. Children will enjoy it too and it's one of the least scary 'ghost' stories that you can read.

The Willows by Algernon Blackwood. Do you dare to read it? This short story is about two campers who pick the wrong place to sleep for the night! Algernon Blackwood is considered a master of the genre.

Other authors of ghost stories to look out for:

- M.R. James

- Edith Wharton

- Bram Stoker

- Walter de la Mare

- Edgar Allen Poe

Pocket Fact 🏕

Many traditional ghost stories are derived from folklore, and became a popular genre during the gothic era in the 19th century.

Reading ghost stories to children

Select ghost stories from well-known children's authors such as Roald Dahl and Philippa Pearce so that you can be sure that the content is suitable. Keep the stories short and finish either with a funny ghost story at the end or another kind of story.

Short and Spooky!: A Book of Very Short Spooky Stories by Louise Cooper. Over 40 stories, each one only two pages long. Some are funny, some scary.

Roald Dahl's Book of Ghost Stories. Master of *Tales of the Unexpected*, Roald Dahl has selected 14 of his favourite classic scary stories – though he has not written the stories himself. One for older children.

Tiny Camper Tip ✏

Remember that young children do need to sleep soundly at night. You won't want them too terrified to go to bed – or even to go camping. Check that they are happy at bedtime and make sure that they have a light with them for night-time use, just in case.

How to make your story more spooky

● Sit around a campfire or some flickering candles.

● If you've got a breeze in the trees or a full moon, incorporate it into your story to make it seem more real.

● Speak in a soft voice and slow down the pace of the story at the really chilling points.

● Speak more loudly and build up towards the end, but give a brief pause just before the punch line.

● Have an 'accomplice' who makes rustling noises or screams (remembering other campers are on site) at appropriate moments.

● Hold a torch under your face.

● Jump up at appropriate moments. You'll find your audience jump too!

Pocket Tip 🔥

If you feel that you cannot tell a ghost story, why not use a professional actor to tell it for you? You can get audiobooks with collections of classic ghost stories, often narrated by familiar names.

⊕ SWIMMING ⊕

Some campsites offer a swimming pool as a facility. At large campsites run by branded companies, these are likely to be fully regulated with lifeguards in attendance. At small campsites, it may be a private pool that is offered simply as an added extra and lifeguards are unlikely to be in attendance.

Before you swim or you let children swim

- Check any rules about timing and only swim at allocated times. The pool is likely to be closed periodically for cleaning or safety.

- Check the water depth before jumping or diving in. It may not be a 'standard' pool with a deep and shallow end, and depths may vary.

- Do not swim alone, and make sure that an adult is in attendance at all times when children are swimming.

- Do not assume other adults will be responsible for your children unless you have made arrangements.

At the seaside

- At campsites next to a beach, make sure that children are supervised and do not let them swim in the sea unaccompanied, however strong a swimmer you feel they may be.

- Check with the campsite owner, manager or other local residents about tides in the area. The conditions may not be suitable for swimming.

- Always tell someone else on the campsite before swimming in the sea.

Pocket Fact 🏕

There are over 300 campsites by the sea or within one mile of a beach in Britain.

7

CAMPING WITH CHILDREN

Camping can be a truly magical experience for little ones that provides a lifetime of rose-tinted memories, and increases the likelihood that one day they will take their own children camping too. Whether you're a seasoned camper yourself or a relative newcomer who wants to introduce your children to the great outdoors at a tender age, this chapter will guide you through the extra preparations and planning you need to make to ensure that children enjoy the experience of camping and embrace it as a life-long hobby.

✸ CAMPING WITH BABIES ✸

When can you start camping with children? That really is all about how comfortable the parents feel rather than any hard and fast rules. Once a baby has been signed off by the midwife, they're ready to go to the great outdoors. That doesn't necessarily mean an arctic adventure, but however simple a trip you're planning to take, you will find that you need to prepare for it in a very different manner. Seasoned campers are much more likely to be confident about venturing out with young babies, but even they will find the familiar activity of camping changes dramatically when you have a baby in tow.

It's perhaps not advisable to venture out on your first-ever camping trip with a young baby. Get to grips with either the camping equipment or the baby first; don't attempt the two together unless you enjoy having a fractious little one and being an irritated parent, trying to feed, change a nappy, and put up a tent for the first time all together. This is not the time for multi-tasking.

Babies are actually quite easy to camp with, providing you go easy on the amount of equipment that you take. Babies can be put into carriers for walking (no dragging of heels just yet!) and placed in carrycots at bedtime.

Tiny Camper Tip ✍

Try camping in early or late summer with a baby. The night-time temperature should still be pleasantly warm but not roasting, and the day times are less likely to be unpleasantly hot for sitting out at a campsite.

You will need to consider the time of year that you camp a little more with a baby or very young child. If they are used to sleeping in a dark bedroom, light coming through the canvas at 4am on a summer's morning could be a rude awakening for you – and them. In these instances, sometimes it's easier to let them get up early, go to bed later, and let them have a sleep sometime during the day. Afternoon naps in a tent are lovely!

✺ CAMPING WITH YOUNG ✺ CHILDREN

Children love an adventure and camping is one of the ultimate adventures for them. The freedom of the great outdoors, sleeping under canvas, cooking and eating in the fresh air all add to the magic of camping when you're a child.

Campsites are one of the best places you can go to for children to meet and play with others – far more than staying at a holiday home. But campsites do have their downsides too: if you want a quiet weekend away to spend some quality time with the children, you may find you've barely seen them as they're so busy making new friends. If this is a worry for you, then you need to decide on the kind of campsite you wish to go to.

Pocket Tip 🔥

If you particularly want to spend time with the children when the excitement of playing with others is there, be firm about mealtimes and make sure that you at least sit down together for an evening meal.

✸ CAMPING WITH TEENAGERS ✸

Only you know your teenagers best and how long they're prepared to continue going on holiday with you! Some may like the space of a farmer's field with not a lot happening, other than a game of Frisbee and a walk to the local shop (and secretly enjoy the family time away from home). Others might need a little more going on, and you could tempt them by staying at a larger campsite where there are likely to be other people of a similar age for them to meet.

Older children are likely to enjoy the independence of sleeping in their own tent and having their own space – you could even add an extra pitch next to yours. Most campsites will not allow unaccompanied children though, so you'll be extremely lucky if you can find a campsite that will let them pitch a tent elsewhere on the site.

Pocket Tip 🔥

Buying a pup tent (see page 8) for older children may be more cost-effective than having to upgrade and buy a larger tent for the whole family.

Enjoy the time with them; soon they'll be backpacking around the world independently. They'll need all the camping skills that you can instil in them then, so try to enjoy your trips together now and don't fret if they want some independence; just try to arrange some activities you can all do as a family (see Chapter 6 for some ideas).

The Scout movement

For many people the epitome of camping, and often their first experience of camping came about as a result of one movement: the Scout and Guides Association.

The founder of the Scout Association was Robert Baden-Powell, a lieutenant-general from the British Army who, in 1907, took some members of the Boys' Brigade for a camping trip on Brownsea Island in Dorset to test out ideas that he was using to write a book for young people on scouting (a concept which arose from Baden-Powell's experience of scouts in the army). Baden-Powell was the vice-president of the Boys' Brigade who were known for their summer camps but Baden-Powell wanted to expand this aspect of the movement. The Boys' Brigade had a religious foundation based on Christian ideals, and initially there was a suggestion of a Scouts Award within this organisation, rather than a separate movement. However, from that initial camping trip at Brownsea Island a separate movement was eventually formed.

Baden-Powell's book Scouting for Boys *was published in 1908 and became one of the bestselling books of the 20th century. His sister Agnes helped him to set up the Girl Guide Association in 1910 after girls gatecrashed the Crystal Palace rally in 1909. Baden-Powell married his wife Olave in 1912 and she became Chief Guide in 1918.*

From that early camping trip both the Scouts and Girl Guides have become synonymous with adventure and camping and are often a child's first experience of camping.

✸ PLANNING YOUR CAMPING TRIP ✸ WITH CHILDREN

Going camping with children does take a little more planning than when you're able to spontaneously pop a rucksack on your back and head off for the hills alone.

DISTANCE TO A CAMPSITE

With a baby you may be able to plan a trip some distance from your home if you know that they will sleep for much of the journey. But don't travel too far from home on your baby's first camping trip, in case there are any problems and you need to return home quickly.

With young children, how far you travel to your selected campsite really depends on your ability to ward off the inevitable, 'Are we there yet?', and if you have planned sufficient activities to keep them occupied for the journey. Again, it's advisable for their very first camping trip to stay relatively close to home – within half an hour or an hour's drive – even if you are an experienced camper. It's all about the camping rather than the travelling the first time round, and if they absolutely hate it, your three-hour drive home could be pretty miserable.

Pocket Tip 🔥

To prevent boredom from setting in on the journey, play a camping version of The Shopping Game, using the alphabet. 'I went to the shop and I bought an airbed; I went to the shop and I bought an airbed and a bottle of gas; I went to the shop and I bought an airbed, a bottle of gas and some cutlery' etc. You never know, it might jog your memory for something you've forgotten to pack! Use the checklist at the back of this book if someone gets stuck for an idea.

LOCATION

Where your campsite is located may turn out to be perfect, or a worrying nightmare. Before booking ask yourself (and the campsite):

- Is the campsite located next to a busy main road without safety barriers at the entrance?

- Are the pitches located next to or near open water?

- Is the campsite located on the side of a hill or mountain with steep drops?

- Is the campsite located next to anything that provides excessive night-time noise that could keep the children awake? (Although invariably, it is the children who will sleep through anything while the adults lie awake all night!)

Pocket Tip 🔥

Remember that in some countries of Europe and on other continents, safety measures are not necessarily as stringent as those in the UK.

None of these things should necessarily stop you from staying at a particular campsite, but at least if you are aware of them you can factor in potential dangers, and possibly ask for a pitch furthest from the main road or river, for example, if you feel it could be a danger to your children.

AT THE CAMPSITE

Routine

Anticipate that your normal routine may well disappear. Part of the fun of camping is getting away from normality, but it may be beneficial to at least stick to some of the routines that your child is used to at home. The times of getting up and going to bed may well be different, but keep the routine the same for any children to get a good night's sleep. If you do things in a certain order at home – bath, teeth, and story at bedtime – stick with that order, even if the actual timing is different.

Tiny Camper Tip 🔦

Encourage your child to take his or her favourite bedtime story to the campsite. The familiarity will be comforting in a strange environment.

Feeding

Think carefully about feeding. Young babies may need bottles or food heated through separately to your own food. Make sure that the campsite has some sort of facilities, or that you provide your own. If you're staying on a larger campsite with its own restaurant, warming bottles and food is not such an issue, but check the opening times coincide with your child's feeding routine.

Toilet training

Think about the development of your baby or child and the stage they are at. Are they in the middle of potty training? It might not be such a good idea to go camping. On the other hand, a week at a campsite, running about outside, can be just the place to attempt daytime potty training. Though night time potty training is not recommended in a tent!

Bathing

Is your child only used to a bath? Be prepared for the fact that most campsites will only have showers and if your child doesn't like them, accept that they may be a bit grubby for a few days and find alternatives if you can – such as a quick scrub down with a wet flannel.

Many of the larger campsites are fully geared up to the needs of babies and children. Even smaller sites are introducing child-friendly camping as they modernise and upgrade their facilities. At all but the tiniest farm campsite, expect at least a changing mat in the toilet block (though you may prefer to take your own towel to place on top for hygiene). Some campsites will provide child steps to reach sinks; others are putting in complete family bathrooms – with a bath – to get that home-from-home experience and make it easier for parents to deal with multiple children at once when washing and bathing.

Plan ahead for eventualities of cold and wet. You're likely to need extra clothing for warmth and, if you have a baby at the crawling stage, to keep clean.

Pocket Tip 🔥

If it's warm and dry and your baby is crawling everywhere, for-get the trousers. You'll find you're doing far less clothes washing if your crawling child wears a pair of shorts instead.

Remember that you are ultimately responsible for your children at a campsite. Camping is all about being able to unwrap children from cotton wool, but if they misbehave, damage property – either accidently or deliberately – injure themselves, or wander off unaccompanied, it is your responsibility.

✸ EQUIPMENT FOR FAMILIES ✸

It can be so tempting to take the contents of your house with you when going on a camping trip with a family, 'just in case'. The boot of your car will determine how much you can take but there are a few items that you will definitely need.

BUGGIES, PUSHCHAIRS, AND CAMPING CHAIRS

Unless you really want to hold or carry the baby every minute of the day, something for them to sit in is a must. You won't have numerous high chairs, sofas, and even clean floors upon which to sit, so a pushchair or buggy can cover numerous jobs – including a high chair for mealtimes.

If you're seasoned campers before the little ones come along and you know that camping will continue with your young family, it pays to set yourself up from the outset with the right gear. So rather than buying a flimsy walking-down-the-pavement-only kind of pushchair first and then feeling the need to double-up with a sturdier all-terrain buggy that will cope with the rigours of camp life, purchase the all-terrain model straight off.

Pocket Tip 🔥

The all-in-one travel systems consisting of a frame on to which you lock a car seat, carrycot, or buggy come into their own on a camping trip. Again, look for one with all-terrain wheels for walks and pushing across campsite fields.

Lightweight camping chairs are not suitable to sit babies and very small children on alone as they can topple over too easily without the weight of an adult. It's better to seat a baby in a pushchair or have them lying on a picnic rug on the ground. However, you can purchase child-size camping chairs in fancy colours and designs that are lower to the ground and therefore less likely to topple over. They are suitable for children from about two to three years old.

SLEEPING AND BEDDING

For young babies a carrycot is the best option in a tent, providing the tent is of a size to accommodate it. You can regulate their temperature better in the carrycot with the use of additional or fewer blankets. Having them in bed with you can be very cosy, but it may be too hot for the baby (especially as you are likely to be warmer than you would be at home), and there is the danger of them becoming smothered by the covers, so save putting the baby in your bed for cuddles in the morning. You'll get a better night's sleep too.

For older babies and toddlers, a folding travel cot is extremely useful when camping. It provides a safe place for them to sleep in the tent and a useful instant playpen in which to put them when you need to do essential jobs, such as erecting the tent and packing everything away at the end of your visit. This does of course mean that you will require a larger, taller tent with more headroom so that the cot does not touch the sides of the tent, or it may become damp.

Children generally love snuggly sleeping bags and you can buy child-size bags that are more appealing than adults'. However, it's critical that you do not put babies of any age into sleeping bags and apply the same rules about putting them to bed at a campsite as you would at home. Baby sleep bags that fit around the child's arms and body so they cannot smother their head are a possibility.

The feet to foot position

- Place the baby at the foot of the carrycot or travel cot, so that their feet touch the end of the cot.

- Make sure that they cannot wriggle themselves underneath the covers and bedclothes.

You may need to provide extra bedding if the outside air is colder than room temperature, bearing in mind that a tent will be draughtier than a bedroom. However, remember that tents can get surprisingly warm, particularly in summer, so a cotton sheet and a blanket may be all that is required when the nights are very warm. The ideal room temperature for a baby to sleep in at home is 16˚C to 20˚C, so aim to stick to the same principles and make sure that there is plenty of ventilation in your tent.

WASHING

Some campsites have the most wonderful washing facilities for families, while others you may prefer to leave well alone. But you're not likely to make friends of other campers if they find you bathing your baby in the washing-up sink.

Pocket Tip 🔥

Bring an inflatable travel baby bath or a flexible 'trug' bucket to bathe your baby at your pitch. A cheap fold-up paddling pool can provide older children with a quick dip before bedtime, though campsite owners will not thank you if you waste their water supplies by filling the pool up to the brim either. An inch or two of water in the bottom with some bath bubbles will suffice.

CLOTHING

- Take extra layers of clothes, in particular for babies, remembering that they will need to be dressed more warmly than you are. Being less mobile, they will become chilled more quickly sitting or lying about at a campsite, so in cooler seasons fleece-lined suits are useful.

- Watch the extremities of feet, hands, and head, and keep these covered up well when it's cold. They'll soon tell you in one way or another if they're feeling uncomfortable! A sunhat is also a must for children of all ages.

- In the summer, children are unlikely to be wearing much more than a t-shirt and a pair of shorts. Keep a jumper for chilly evenings though if they're going to join you around the campfire (try stopping them!).

- Take a pair of waterproof trousers and a cagoule for muddy weather. Wear these over clothes and you'll save on the amount of clothes you need to take and on the washing you'll need to do.

- If children are going on any kind of lengthy walk, a pair of good fitting trainers or walking shoes are better than sandals, flip-flops, or pumps, which will provide them with a good set of blisters in no time.

WHAT TOYS TO BRING (AND WHAT TO LEAVE AT HOME!)

Children like to feel secure and, given the chance, will pack up much of their bedroom to take with them on a camping trip. Set a limit, perhaps by providing them with an appropriate sized bag and insisting that anything that will not fit in won't be going.

- If you can, try to tempt them away from bringing lots of electronic devices. Safety of your/their equipment (theft, getting wet, lost, or damaged) needs much greater consideration when camping than in a locked hotel room or your own accommodation. Besides, camping is all about interaction and getting out in the fresh air, rather than hiding in the car with headphones on.

- It's best to avoid taking any items that are either financially valuable or of immense sentimental value. Losing it is just not worth the hassle.

- A football is always a good addition if there is space in your luggage. It's a great ice-breaker for playing with other children on the campsite and a good opportunity for a run around if energy needs to be lost before bedtime.

- Let them take a teddy bear or soft toy that feels comforting, but insist that an entire zoo is not required. There simply won't be room in the tent (or car) and it's yet another item that could get lost.

- Check with the campsite before loading up bikes, scooters, rollerblades, and skateboards. Some won't allow them to be ridden around the camping ground for safety reasons and unless you're planning on going for a bike ride off-site, you're wasting valuable space.

Pocket Tip 🔥

Check any rules on the campsite. Some don't allow ball games around the pitches, but there will usually be a play area allocated if that's the case.

✳ ACTIVITIES ✳

The kind of campsite that you stay at may determine the sorts of activities that you can do. The very largest campsites – more like holiday parks where you're staying for a fortnight – tend to have several children's activities laid on with entertainers at certain times of the day. They may also have a 'kids club' or a crèche to look after little ones. At these and any other large sites, however, the best activities are those you can do and play with little or no specialist equipment other than the things you would expect to have with you for a camping trip. These can encourage children to use some ingenuity and a little bit of imagination too.

Treasure/scavenger hunts

Prepare a list (as long or short as you like, depending on the time available or the attention span and age of the children) of items to search for and collect. Make sure that some are easier to find than others. These could include: a seed or nut, a feather, a rubbing from the bark of a tree (paper and crayons required), a pine cone, a small pebble, the leaf from a particular bush, a fruit such as a blackberry or a crab apple in autumn, and fallen blossom in spring. This can be played with a camera too for proof, in which case you can add in alternatives such as a ladybird or beetle, a church spire, or a cowpat!

You can make this activity harder by asking for examples of, 'the thinnest twig, the prickliest object, the smoothest object, the tiniest pebble' etc.

Simple map reading and route-finding games

Discovering map reading at an early age will help children immensely with activities in later life. Ditch the GPS and pull out a good old-fashioned Ordnance Survey map. Look at what all the symbols mean, try to match them up with the area in which you're staying (such as a church, telephone box or pub), and show them how to make a plan of the campsite. Then try some simple orienteering.

Pocket Fact

Geocaching is like a giant treasure hunt nationwide, and is certainly one that older children will appreciate as it's a bit more sophisticated than a standard treasure hunt. You'll need a GPS system to locate the various treasure chests (called caches) that are dotted about the countryside. When you find the caches, you can take out a souvenir but you must replace it with something else ready for the next person to find. Caches are listed on geocaching websites such as www.geocaching.com.

Nature studies

Use the outdoors to the best advantage by looking at things such as the night-sky to identify stars, rockpooling along the coast, or identifying trees through a walk in the woods. What to look out for is listed in Chapter 6 of this book but, for starters, try the easiest of everything – such as the Great Bear star constellation (look for a giant saucepan in the sky), a holly tree with prickly leaves, and a limpet clinging to the rocks at the seaside.

Calming down

Have an idea ready for a quiet sitting-down activity for when it's too hot to rush around or it's time to calm down. Try:

- Showing them how to tie different kinds of knots (although it could get very frustrating); you never know when they could be useful. Always supervise children with ropes for safety reasons.

- Making up a collective story where one person begins a sentence and the next person finishes it off. For example, the first person begins, 'There was once a man . . .' The next person continues the sentence, '. . . who had very knobbly knees and one whisker growing from the end of his chin . . .' and so it goes on. It can be silly or compelling, but no one knows how it's going to end!

- Encircle a small area of grass (or ground in the woods) with a piece of string and sit quietly to see how many bugs, insects and worms are in the circle.

- Provide the children with a long word and ask them to find other words using the letters.

Pocket Tip 🔥

Pack a small activity box yourself for the children – a pack of playing cards, pens and paper (in a pad or with something to rest on so it doesn't blow about the campsite), or a travel games compendium. Have it easily accessible so that as soon as you arrive at the campsite they can sit quietly while you unpack and pitch the tent (if they're not going to be involved in the immediate chores).

✦ WALKING ✦

Babies

Babies can be placed in a carrier so cause few problems when going for a hike (providing you get the right one, to prevent you from having back ache). They'll enjoy the fresh air and the ability to look at things as you walk – a much slower speed than in a car, where their eyes cannot focus on objects quickly enough.

Toddlers

Toddlers are tricky on longer walks; anything much over a mile and you'll have a dragging of heels and a request to be carried – hard work for you. Consider an all-terrain buggy if you wish to do some halfway decent walking on anything but a pavement and for some distance.

Young children

From the age of five years, children are more capable of walking greater distances. Many five year olds are quite capable of a four- to five-mile-walk, providing the terrain is relatively easy and there is plenty of scenery to keep them interested.

As soon as you can, get them more involved in the walk by giving them a small, lightweight backpack to carry (not stuffed full so it's too heavy, or you'll end up carrying it), or giving help with map reading.

Teenagers

Teenagers should be quite capable of walking as far as an adult. Find an interesting route with plenty of opportunities for other activities such as orienteering and geocaching (see page 158).

Pocket Tip 🔥

Remember to take plenty of water for everyone and a snack to maintain energy levels, such as a cereal bar, piece of fruit, or bag of boiled sweets.

✦ ENCOURAGING CHILDREN TO ✦ ENJOY CAMPING

Children probably won't need much encouragement to enjoy going on a camping trip, providing they don't have bad memories of a previous trip that went disastrously wrong. They will not enjoy their camping experience if they:

- Get cold (the most common reason for putting children off the outdoors) and have no way of warming up

- Get wet (and cold) and don't have the right clothing or footwear for the activities

- Get scared at night

- Get overly hungry

One way to encourage a life-long love of camping is to allow them to become involved.

HOW CHILDREN CAN HELP

Children generally love to get involved with jobs around the campsite and there's plenty that they can help with too:

- Fetching and carrying water

- Taking rubbish to the bins

- Buying fresh bread from the campsite shop in the morning

- Laying out their bedding in the tent upon arrival

Helping with the washing and drying up is a good one too (why else do campers use plastic plates and cups?!) If you're lucky, you'll come across the campsites that provide child-height washing-up areas to ensure the little ones do their share of the chores.

While it's important to get young children involved, it's even more important to let teenage children get in on the action. Give them some responsibility and put them in charge of the cooking or making the campfire – something that they won't see as a menial task.

Pocket Fact 🏕

Some campsites may allow children to help with other tasks too such as collecting eggs from a chicken coop, helping to feed some animals, or watering plants. Jobs they usually shy away from at home suddenly become a lot more interesting on a campsite!

SAFETY PRECAUTIONS TO TAKE

Part of the fun of camping is allowing children that extra bit of freedom to explore by themselves, while still maintaining their safety.

It may sound overly cautious, but if you're camping with a baby or young child, take a few minutes before or when you arrive to ascertain where the nearest doctor and hospital is. The campsite reception should be able to tell you this. Then put the information to the back of your mind and enjoy your camping trip. At least then, should an emergency arise, you can save precious minutes.

If you go off for a walk together, set some guidelines before you leave about children being by themselves. Don't let them go on ahead if there is a fork coming up in the footpath or, if there is, ensure that they know to wait until you arrive rather than carry on blindly. Make sure that they know to sit and wait every few minutes rather than continue on ahead regardless. If need be, arm them with a whistle that's only to be blown in the event of an emergency.

Pocket Tip 🔥

Two-way radios are good for use with children either on a walk or on the campsite — you can call them back or locate them when needed. Mobile phones don't always work, especially if you're in the depths of the countryside.

If the campsite or pitch is next to a pond, stream, river, or lake, take extra precautions with young children and consider requesting an alternative pitch if you're not confident with the location. You will not be able to relax if you're always wondering if they're safe.

Campsites are usually very friendly places and children love to meet new people and make friends. They're also the sorts of places that we tend to relax and drop our guard. But it's a sad world that we sometimes live in and campsites are full of strangers. Don't go overboard on the precautions, but remind your children that if there is anyone that they feel uncomfortable about being around, to tell you.

Camping books for children

Try reading these classic camping stories with your children to get them excited for the trip:

- Little House on the Prairie *by Laura Ingalls Wilder. Camping across America in a tented wagon.*
- Five Go Off in a Caravan *by Enid Blyton. Classic camping adventure story.*
- Camping Out (The Pyjama Gang) *by P.J. Denton. One of the group needs to overcome their fear of creepy crawlies in this adventure from the Pyjama Gang.*

8

FESTIVAL CAMPING

The party is in full swing, the music's jumping, and the ground is thumping to the sound of partygoers dancing to the beat. It's festival time.

Not all festivals involve music of course, but they do have one thing in common: camping. There the similarity ends because, depending on the festival, your camping experience may be rolling your cheap, 'It'll last for one-night-only' tent up into a ball of mud, or quaffing champagne from your chic boutique tent having flown in by private helicopter. Or maybe it will be something in between. Whatever type of festival experience you're going for, this chapter will guide you through a few basic tips to make sure it's an enjoyable one.

✳ IS IT CAMPING? ✳

It's not really possible to say that camping at a festival is anything like 'camping' elsewhere; that is, camping at a campsite or wild camping.

- With wild camping, it's you, maybe a couple of bears, and a view as far as the eye can see.

- At a campsite, it's you, a few other campers, and maybe the sea.

- At a festival, it's you, twenty thousand other campers, and a sea of tents as far as the eye can see.

There will be hundreds if not thousands of 'campers' at a festival who have never been camping before in their lives – and are never likely to again. It is the festival that they are going for, and pitching up in a tent happens to be the way to live relatively cheaply for a weekend so as not to miss the action.

There are of course thousands of festival-goers who are going for the whole festival experience – including the camping – but it is still a very different form of 'camping'. However, that doesn't mean it has to be a terrible experience; it just requires a different kind of planning to 'traditional' camping.

✿ HOW TO SELECT YOUR PITCH ✿

Festivals that span out over several fields usually have many different options for camping. Once you have decided on the event that you wish to attend, have a look on the festival website and look at the camping details. You need to make sure that when you book your tickets for the event, you select the campsite option that suits you best. If you're going with friends and you want to camp together, make sure they book the same camping option too, or you could find yourself fields apart – and that could be a lengthy walk.

The kinds of camping options that are often available at festivals include:

- General one-size-fits-all camping areas for tents, with a car

- Car-free camping areas for tents

- Camping area for motorhomes, caravans, and campervans

- A family area for quiet(er) camping

- Late-night parties camping area

- Disabled camping area

Then there are the alternative 'camping' areas, which are proving more popular and bigger business every year. For these you don't need to be in possession of a tent at all. Again, depending on which festival you visit, you can choose to stay in:

- A tepee (or tipi)

- A yurt

- A camping pod
- A safari tent
- A Bedouin tent
- A bell tent
- A gypsy caravan
- A retro campervan
- A retro Airstream caravan
- . . . and anything else that organisers can come up with in the meantime

All of these options will have a different ambience so think carefully about the type of experience you want to have before making your choice.

The VW Campervan

First introduced in 1950, the VW Bus/Campervan became extremely popular with campers during the Swinging Sixties. The first models had a split-windscreen: an iconic piece of design which was changed to a bay window in 1967.

They've attracted a cult following ever since, with VW campervan rallies held worldwide. In recent years, their popularity has boomed with their colourful paintwork and distinctive engine noise endearing themselves to a new generation, and making campervans an enduring icon at festivals all over Britain. In 2010 the VW Campervan celebrated its 60th anniversary and it looks as if it is here to stay.

FINDING YOUR PITCH

Finding your pitch will depend on the campsite that you have chosen. Most operate an organised free-for-all; that is, you hand over your ticket at the entrance gate and marshals will direct you to a car park. From there you walk to the particular camping area in which you have selected to erect your tent. Once in the camping area you can generally pitch your tent anywhere you like, and by the time everyone has pitched their tent, you will see more canvas than grass. There is generally no set pitch size and tents can get a little cosy side by side.

Alternatively, if it is a festival where you can camp with your car, the marshals will position cars and campervans in the same way as they do in a car park, and they will probably ask you to pitch in an orderly fashion in front of or to one side of your car. You may or may not be able to camp with your car, but that depends upon each festival and the licence that they have for camping.

This is something to bear in mind if you anticipate being able to leave bedding to stay dry or valuables safe in your vehicle. You may also have a long, long walk from the car or bus-stop to the camping areas.

Top five tips to select the best pitch

1. You may like the idea of it being convenient to nip to the loo in the night, but don't pitch your tent too close to the toilets. You could have people tripping over your tent all night long, and despite the best efforts of organisers, they can pong!

2. If you wish to get some sleep at some point – particularly during the day – find a pitch or tent area that is slightly further away from any of the stages.

3. Quiet camping areas are meant to be just that. Don't pitch there if you intend to party all night.

4. Likewise, if you enjoy your beauty sleep and want to be quiet, don't expect everyone else to be if you've pitched your tent in a 'rowdy' field.

5. One of the safest places to camp is close to a steward's contact point. They're usually on duty 24 hours a day so someone in charge will always be about.

At most festivals, every camping field has a marshal in charge of that area. They will be your first point of contact for anything in connection with camping, including finding a pitch.

Pocket Fact 🏕

Some festivals allow campers who arrive on foot or by bike to camp for free.

⊛ RULES AND REGULATIONS ⊛

Every festival has a set of rules and regulations. They should be clearly signposted on site, will often be on the festival website, and may well be on the back of your ticket.

The rules are there for your safety first and foremost, but also so that festival organisers can abide by the laws of the land and any conditions that may be imposed upon them in order to be granted a licence to hold the event. If the organisers cannot uphold these conditions, the event may be closed down and you won't have a festival to go to.

Festivals can accommodate anything from a few hundred people to 140,000 people. That's a big-tented town, so it is important that festival-goers abide by the rules imposed. The results of someone deciding to light a sparkler in their tent or peeing in the nearby stream could be catastrophic.

Rules that regularly crop up at festivals are:

- No drugs
- No selling anything without a licence provided by organisers
- No fireworks or flares
- Food and alcohol brought on site must be for personal consumption only
- No glass bottles

Pocket Tip 🔥

Some events may make a rule of it, but it is generally recommended that you don't take pets to a festival, particularly one with loud music. Aside from the welfare of the pet, there are health and safety implications for festival-goers too.

✳ ESSENTIAL FESTIVAL EQUIPMENT ✳

There are some must-haves at a festival and some need-nots.

These are the must-haves:

- Tent (unless you're staying in alternative accommodation). If you're unfamiliar with camping, try getting a pop-up tent that does exactly that as it comes out of its protective bag. You can get them in funky designs, manufactured specifically with festival-goers in mind

- Rucksack (see page 26). Worthwhile if you're arriving by car, as you could have some distance to walk from a car pack to the camping field

- Sleeping mat and bedding

- Towel and personal toiletries, including sun cream

- A small first aid kit

- Torch (and spare batteries)

- Waterproof coat and trousers

- Wellies (and some alternative footwear too)

- Clothing (including a fleece in case it gets chilly)

- Bags for dirty clothing/wellies

- Festival ticket

Pocket Tip 🔥

Keep some clean clothes just for going home in. They might take up a bit of room but you'll really appreciate it after a few days of muddy camping!

Extras that may be worth taking:

- Wheelbarrow or sled for transporting your equipment, children etc from the car to the campsite

- Ear plugs

- Wet wipes (useful for so many things, not just changing a baby's nappy!)

- Hangover cure

- Contraceptives

Pocket Tip 🔥

If you find you have forgotten something when you arrive, many festivals sell camping equipment – including tents!

What not to take:

- Glass. Very few festivals will allow glass on site and it may well be confiscated if searched at the entrance. Make sure that any drinks are in plastic containers and any baby foods you may be taking are not packaged in glass jars. Don't forget an empty plastic bottle for water.

- Fireworks, flares, firelighters

- Pets

- Valuables

- Anything that you really don't need for a weekend

FOOD TO TAKE

You can take cooking equipment and food with you. However, if you feel it is yet another thing to carry, many festivals have plenty of opportunities to purchase food – everything from yogurt and smoothie bars for breakfast, to international cuisine such as curries and burgers.

You'll be able to buy foods to cook with too, so you only need to take the cooking equipment. Unless your aim is to be cooking gourmet dinners, a single-burner stove should suffice for a weekend.

Pocket Tip 🔥

As well remembering everything you need to take to the festival, you should also remember at the end to take everything away that you arrived with – including your tent. Tents can be bought so cheaply these days that some people are inclined to leave theirs behind; it's just plain rude and the clear-up operation will cost you more on the price of your ticket next year.

Funky festival equipment suppliers

- *www.onestopfestival.com*
- *www.funkyleisure.co.uk*
- *www.festivalcamping.co.uk*

Don't forget that many high street camping shops also sell equipment for festival camping.

✴ FESTIVAL SURVIVAL GUIDE ✴

MUD, WASHING, AND TOILET ISSUES

We've all seen the images on the television of mud, mud, glorious mud. Why is it that a festival campsite attracts storm clouds like a magnet does iron?

Take wellies but don't use them if you can get away with it. They'll make your feet sweat horribly if you wear them constantly for several days – not to mention how smelly it can all get around the toes.

Showers are busiest first thing in the morning. Try taking an afternoon shower when there's less pressure on the facilities and less likelihood of queuing. If the showers are fully occupied, too horrible to use, or just too far to go to, have a strip wash in your tent using biodegradable wet wipes or a wet flannel.

Bushes, hedges, streams, and ditches are not the place for toilet activities. However, the loos may be too far to reach at night, so take a small bucket with a tight fitting lid (composting buckets or portable potties can do the trick) for night-time use. Just remember to empty it first thing in the morning or it will become a health issue.

FINDING YOUR TENT AGAIN

In order to find your tent you need to know where it is in the first place. Pitch your tent and unpack your equipment before drinking any alcohol. You'll then be able to gather your bearings, be aware of notable landmarks and their position in relation to your tent, and you'll be more likely to have a tent that you can actually crawl into without tangled guy ropes.

Mark or personalise your tent or pitch in some way with a notable feature, remembering that once everyone else has also marked their pitch with a similar looking flag, yours might not be so distinguishable. Why not be inventive and make up your own flag design using all of your friend's initials?

FINDING YOUR FRIENDS AND FAMILY AGAIN

Mobile phones are the obvious solution if you become separated from a group, but just in case they don't work or run out of battery, it's a good idea to agree on a central meeting point when you first arrive.

Select a location for a meeting point in emergencies, such as outside a particular steward's office or underneath a certain flagpole.

It can be overwhelming for children to become lost, never mind the frantic worry for parents. Arm them with some basic safety advice without alarming them and arrange an easily-recognisable meeting place close to wherever you are at the time.

Place a wristband (the kind that can't come off without cutting it) on their arm and write your mobile telephone number on it. Don't include the child's name though.

If you're parting company with friends for a while, arrange a specific time when you all 'touch base' again, even if it's contact by phone.

✦ STAYING SAFE ✦

Keeping your belongings safe is important, but keeping yourself and those around you safe takes priority.

How to look after yourself

- Wash your hands often, especially before eating, to reduce the risk of food poisoning. A tiny bottle of antibacterial gel is useful to keep with you at all times.

- It may be common sense, but make sure that you eat well and get a good amount of sleep – even if it's at abnormal times.

- Keep drinking plenty of water – especially if you are drinking alcohol.

- Be aware of the sun and heat – keep slapping on the sun cream and wear a trendy sun hat.

- Be considerate to your ears and take rest breaks for them away from the noise of music and hullabaloo.

- Look out for others and they will hopefully do the same for you.

- If camping with a group, make sure everyone has a role to play (to avoid arguments). For example: pitching the tent, cooking, rubbish collector, water carrier, etc.

In an emergency

Contact a festival steward or marshal first. You are likely to receive attention much quicker than dialling 999 and trying to explain where you are (and the emergency services being able to reach you).

Keeping your belongings safe

- The easy answer to this is not to take anything that you can do without on site. Some festivals provide secure property lock-ups. Use them if you need to; it will be considerably safer than your tent or your car.

- Write your postcode on any valuables with a UV pen. If your mobile phone or camera is lost rather than stolen, festival officials will have more chance of returning the item to you.

- Say 'hello' to your campsite neighbours. You'll get to know familiar faces that should be around your camping area and can look out for one another's property.

- Tents are vulnerable and there is unfortunately no way of securing them. A padlock on the zip simply says you've got something worth having and it takes seconds for the opportunist to get in. Don't leave anything of value in them, including sentimental items.

- If you are unfortunate in losing possessions, make a campsite steward your first port of call. They can notify relevant staff.

- Don't bring items that could be lost easily – leave your house keys with a good neighbour or friend rather than taking them to the festival.

- Put your money and valuables in inventive places such as in your sock, at the base of your wellies, or in your bra – but not all in the same place!

- Neither should you rely on leaving valuables in a car, even hidden away. Your car could be parked in a field some distance away and while festival sites are 'policed', they can't check over every single car all of the time.

Pocket Tip 🔥

Rather than take a very expensive camera, take a cheap disposable, a cheap digital (you can still get reasonable quality pictures from a relatively inexpensive camera), or rely on your mobile phone.

9

CAMPING CHECKLIST

Use this list to help you with your packing.

✦ PACKING LIST ✦

EQUIPMENT

Tent (check all parts are correct and in place)

Extensions, such as a porch

Additional pup tent

Spare guy ropes, poles, and tent pegs

Mallet

Tent repair kit (gaffer tape, seam sealant, cable ties, glue, scissors, patch kit)

Groundsheet (for beneath tent and for porch area)

Internal groundsheet (or picnic rug if you're using this instead)

SLEEPING

Sleeping mats, airbeds, or campbeds

Bedding (sleeping bags, liners, duvets, airbed sheets, blankets, pillows)

Airbed pump

COOKING

Camping stove

Camping kitchen (if you're taking one)

Gas

Barbecue

Barbecue lighting fuel/charcoal

Matches

Pans

Coolbox or camping fridge

Freezer blocks

Toaster (low-wattage)

Kettle (gas or low-wattage)

Plates

Mugs

Glasses (plastic)

Cutlery

Other utensils (wooden spoons, cheese grater, preparation knives, chopping board)

Cooking foil

Serving/salad bowl

Water bottles/carriers

Water purification tablets

Kitchen towel

LIVING

Chairs

Table

Rugs

Torch

Camping lantern (plus gas)

Electric hook-up extension lead (and adaptors)

Portable toilet (plus toilet tent and chemical liquid)

Rucksack and/or daysack

Storage boxes

Trug bucket

CLOTHING

Underwear (thermal if necessary) and base-layer leggings

Trousers

Shorts

Fleece jumpers/jacket

Waterproof cagoule

Waterproof trousers

Socks/walking socks

Hiking boots

Wellington boots

Lightweight footwear (eg flip-flops)

Pyjamas

Sunhat

Warm hat, gloves, scarf

Sunglasses

PERSONAL TOILETRIES

Toilet roll

Solar shower (if you want one)

Towels and flannels

Sun cream

Hot water bottle

Antibacterial dry hand wash

Soap/shampoo

Toothbrush/paste

Wet wipes

First aid kit (antihistamine cream, antiseptic cream, plasters, painkillers, bandages)

Mosquito repellent

⊛ FOOD ⊛

Pet food

Tea, coffee, hot chocolate

Sugar

Salt and pepper

Stock cubes

Tinned beans

Ketchup, chutney

Pasta

Rice

Jam

Cereal

Milk (to get you started)

First night's supper (pre-prepared)

Marshmallows

⊛ ACTIVITES AND GAMES ⊛

Board games

Books

Field guide

Football

Playing cards

Badminton or tennis rackets

⊛ CHILDREN ⊛

Pushchair or buggy

Baby carrier

Carrycot or travel cot

Travel bath

Activity pack (paper, pens, crayons etc)

Bedtime stories

Walkie-talkies

⊛ TRAVEL DOCUMENTATION ⊛

The Camping Pocket Bible

Campsite guidebook

Maps

Emergency telephone numbers

Campsite booking confirmation

Tickets (ferry, aeroplane, train, railcard)

Club membership card

Camping Card International

Passport (if camping internationally)